VALOR

Swords

Valor. ed. by Isabelle Melançon and Megan Lavey-Heaton
300 pages

Printed in Canada

Second Printing, 2019

ISBN 978-0-9853-0957-2 (hardback)
ISBN 978-0-9853-0958-9 (paperback)

1. Fairy tales--Adaptations. 2. Folklore--Adaptations. 3. Heroines in literature. 4. Short stories. 5. Graphic novels. I. Title.

GR470.V35 2015
398.2'082--dc23

Fairylogue Press
4173 Grouse Ct. #115
Mechanicsburg, PA 17050

www.fairyloguepress.com

VALOR

Fairy tales do not inform children that there is such things as monsters. Children already know that there are monsters. What fairy tales really teach is that monsters can be transformed or destroyed.

– Paraphrasing
G.K. Chesterton

TABLE OF CONTENTS

Prunella

Story by Megan Lavey-Heaton and Isabelle Melançon
Art by Isabelle Melançon

MEDDLESOME BRATS!
GET AWAY FROM THOSE FRUIT TREES!
OR I'LL TEACH YOU A LESSON YOU WON'T FORGET!
NO!

YOU AGAIN?
FOOLISH GIRL, YOU THINK I HAVEN'T SEEN YOU STEAL BEFORE?
NO, PLEASE!
I'M SO HUNGRY!

MOTHER!
LET ME GO!
YOU THINK YOU CAN STEAL FROM WITCHES?
YOU'RE NOT A REAL PERSON ANYWAY!

IS THAT SO?
THEN HEED THIS CURSE.
YOU SHALL BE KNOWN AS PRUNELLA. BRAINS AND BEAUTY YOU WILL HAVE, BUT THE WORLD WILL FIND YOUR NAME REPULSIVE!

IN A VILLAGE NEAR THE RIVER, THERE LIVED A GIRL CALLED PRUNELLA. SHE USED TO HAVE ANOTHER NAME, BUT WHEN SHE WAS A CHILD, THE WITCH OF THE TREES TOOK HER NAME.

STUPID WITCH.

STUPID BIRDS.

THIS CURSE CAUSED PEOPLE TO BE SCARED OF PRUNELLA AND REFUSE TO GIVE HER WORK. THANKFULLY, PRUNELLA WASN'T SCARED OF EITHER THE WITCH OF THE TREES OR HER SISTER, THE WITCH OF THE WINDS.

STUPID STAIRS.

BANG!
BANG!

WHO *DARES* TO INTRUDE UPON MY ... OH IT'S *YOU* AGAIN
THAT'S RIGHT. YOU OWE ME A JOB.
WHY?
BECAUSE YOU *CURSED* ME!
YOU ATE MY PLUMS!
I WAS *SIX YEARS OLD!*

I DON'T LIKE YOU ...
... BUT I DO NEED A MAID.

HERE.
FILL THIS WITH WATER AND YOU'LL HAVE A JOB.

THIS IS A WICKER BASKET.

WITH A BIG *HOLE* IN IT!

SLAM

OF ALL THE ...

GOOD MORNING, DEAR PRUNELLA! NEED ANY HELP?

I'LL GLADLY PROVIDE IT IN EXCHANGE FOR A KISS.
FORGET IT, BEE'S BREATH

I'LL *NEVER* KISS THE SON OF A WITCH!
ESPECIALLY ONE THAT FORGETS TO TELL HIS FRIENDS ABOUT HIS CRAZY MOTHER AND HER CURSES!
STILL MAD AFTER ALL THESE YEARS, HUH?

GEE,
YOU THINK?

I CAN DO THIS *MYSELF!*

FLAK!

A WEEK LATER ...

THIS WAS A *TERRIBLE* IDEA.

GIRL! GET IN HERE!

BAKE ME SOME BREAD FOR A SPELL!
MAKE SURE IT'S READY WHEN I RETURN FROM MY SISTER'S OR *ELSE*!

WITH WHAT INGREDIENTS?
SLAM

HEY, I JUST HAPPENED TO GRAB THIS BREAD IN THE VILLAGE THIS MORNING. WANT IT?

ASSUMING YOU WANT TO KEEP YOUR JOB.
I DO!
WELL, I DON'T, BUT I DO!

WAIT.
DO I HAVE TO KISS YOU FOR THIS?

A KISS WOULD BE NICE ...
NOT A CHANCE! BUT THANKS, BENSIABEL!

AND SO, TRIAL AFTER TRIAL WAS IMPOSED ON POOR PRUNELLA DURING HER WEEKS OF EMPLOYMENT.

TABITHA! CEASE THOSE INFERNAL WINDS THIS INSTANT!

AS YOU WISH ...

... DEAR AGATHA.

...
I'VE COME TO END OUR FEUD AND DIVIDE MOTHER'S JEWELS!
BE A GOOD SISTER AND LET ME HAVE SOME OF YOUR DELICIOUS FRUIT IN A PIE?

GIRL!
I'M COMING, I'M COMING!

OH NO ...

WHAT IS IT? CAN I HELP?
I LOST IT! WHERE IS IT?

GIRL! GET OVER HERE! NOW!

JUST A SECOND!

NOW!
OR I WILL CHANGE YOU INTO A TOAD!

YOU TOO, BENSIABEL!

I DO HAVE A NAME YOU KNOW.
A HORRIBLE ONE.
WHOSE FAULT IS THAT?
OH, GO GET FRUIT TO MAKE A PIE. MAKE SURE IT HAS WORMS.
BEN, GO TO THE KITCHEN AND STAY THERE UNTIL I TELL YOU OTHERWISE.

MOTHER, I ...
DON'T ARGUE. YOUR AUNT IS HERE, AND ALL SHE NEEDS IS ONE DISTRACTION TO MESS THINGS UP.

BEN?
ARE YOU OK?

IT'S WARM ...

WELL, THE OVEN'S LIT.
WANT ME TO GET YOU SOME WATER?

BEN?

WHAT'S THIS?

GIRL!
WHERE'S THAT PIE?

VOILA. ONE PIE. HOPE YOU CHOKE.
YOU'D THINK LOSING YOUR NAME WOULD TEACH YOU HUMILITY.
INDEED.
BUT NOPE.

BON APPETIT!

WAIT ... STOP ...
PLEASE ... STOP HER.
BEN?
MUNCH MUNCH MUNCH

ONE OF THE PLUMS IN THE PIE IS ENCHANTED ...

BEN'S HEART!

GET BEHIND ME, PRUNELLA!
YOU DIDN'T THINK I'D FIND OUT ABOUT HOW YOU ENCHANTED A PLUM TO CREATE A SON, THEN HID YOUR POWERS IN HIS HEART?
I USED MY WINDS TO STEAL HIS HEART! YOU MADE IT SO EASY! NOW I RULE OVER THE WIND AND THE TREES!

SO MUCH FOR TREE POWERS! AND NOW ...

GET OUT!

I'LL BE BACK, SISTER! YOUR DEMONIC SERVANT DOESN'T SCARE ME!

I'LL BE WAITING!

PRUNELLA, YOU ...
BEN!

DON'T WORRY. MOTHER WILL FIX ME RIGHT UP.
I'M SO SORRY I BAKED YOUR HEART INTO A PIE!

I OWED YOU A KISS FOR THAT.

AHEM.
THE KITCHEN STILL NEEDS CLEANING.

Little Fish

By Emily Hann

Based on The Little Mermaid
by Hans Christian Andersen

THE DAY SHE CAME FROM THE OCEAN...
... HOW COULD I HAVE KNOWN WHAT THAT REALLY MEANT?

GASP

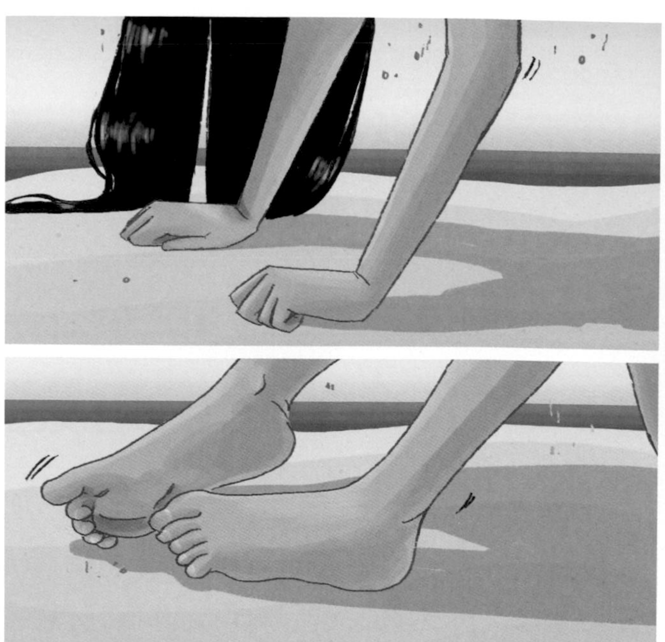

WHAT'S THIS? A LITTLE FISH THAT FLOPPED OUT OF THE OCEAN?

THE BOTTOM OF THE OCEAN WAS COLD.
AND HER COLD MERMAID FAMILY SHUNNED HER AFFECTION.

WHERE DID YOU COME FROM FROM?
WHAT'S YOUR NAME?
WHAT HAPPENED TO YOU?

PARDON ME, MY PRINCE.

SHE'S MUTE - SHE CAN'T SPEAK.
MY MOTHER'S DEAF, I'VE USED SIGN LANGUAGE SINCE I WAS A CHILD.
IF I CAN TEACH THE GIRL THE BASICS, MAYBE SHE CAN TELL US WHO SHE IS.
THAT'S FINE, JUST MAKE SURE YOU HOLD THE LESSONS ON YOUR OWN TIME SO THEY WON'T INTERFERE WITH YOUR WORK.

COME NOW.

FRUIT.
FRUIT.
FRUIT.
TO EAT.
EAT.
EAT.
FISH.
DAUGHTER.

AFTER A FEW LESSONS, SHE WANTED TO SHOW THE PRINCE WHAT SHE COULD DO.

I'LL NEVER BE ABLE TO UNDERSTAND YOU, LITTLE FISH. BUT PLEASE KEEP BEING SO ENTERTAINING.
WHY DON'T YOU DANCE FOR ME?

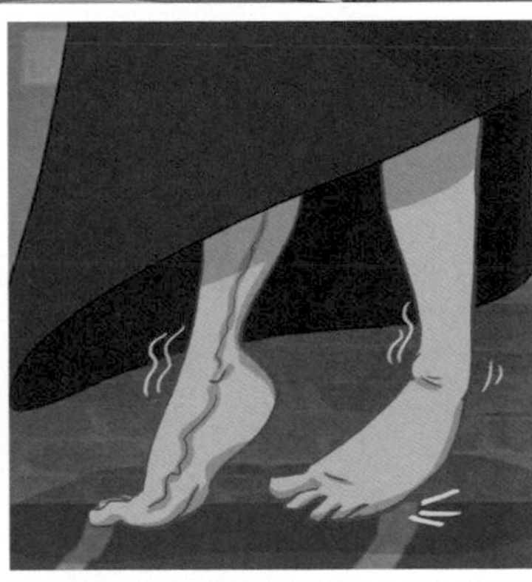

HE HAD LEFT IN THE MIDDLE OF THE DANCE.
DON'T WORRY. IT'S GOING TO BE OKAY.
LET US HELP.

...AND DIDN'T SEEM TO CARE AT ALL.

I NEED TO TELL THE PRINCE SOMETHING IMPORTANT.

NEED...

LIKE WHAT?

IT LOOKS LIKE A WEDDING TENT...

LITTLE FISH, I REALLY WANT YOU TO MEET SOMEONE.

THIS IS MY BRIDE.
I WISH YOU COULD TELL ME HOW HAPPY YOU ARE FOR US, BUT I CAN SEE IT UPON YOUR FACE.

WHY ARE YOU SO UPSET?
ME.
I DON'T UNDER-STAND.

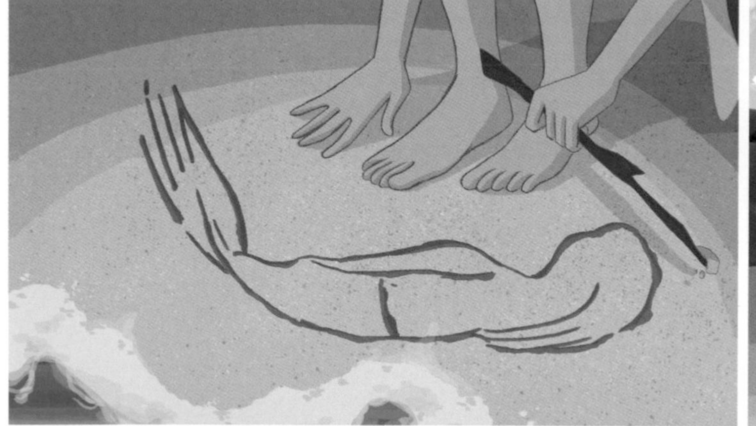

ME.

I USED MAGIC TO COME OUT OF THE OCEAN, AND I NEEDED TO GAIN THE LOVE OF A HUMAN TO STAY HERE.
NOW THAT THE PRINCE WILL BE MARRIED, I WILL RETURN TO THE SEA AS THE FOAM ON THE WAVES.
I WILL DIE.

NO.

The end.

Bride of the Rose Beast

BY MICHELLE "MISHA" KRIVANEK

I NEVER KNEW THAT MY WEDDING NIGHT WOULD BE THIS DANGEROUS...
LYE
MILK

SIGH

NO MATTER WHAT HAPPENS....
I MUST BE READY...

ONCE UPON A TIME, THERE WAS A HAPPY KINGDOM, EXCEPT FOR ONE PROBLEM...
THE KING AND QUEEN OF THE LAND HAD NO CHILD OF THEIR OWN.

ONE DAY, THE SAD QUEEN WENT ON A WALK THROUGH THE WOODS.

YOUR MAJESTY?

YOU LOOK TROUBLED, MY DEAR. WHAT IS WRONG?
OH, IT'S NO USE. YOU COULDN'T HELP ME EVEN IF I TOLD YOU.
TRY ME,
I MAY SURPRISE YOU.

SIGH... WELL, THE KING AND I HAVE NO CHILD OF OUR OWN.
THAT IS WHY I AM TROUBLED.

IS THAT ALL? I HAVE JUST THE SOLUTION, MY LOVE.
TONIGHT, TAKE A CUP WITH TWO HANDLES TO YOUR GARDEN.

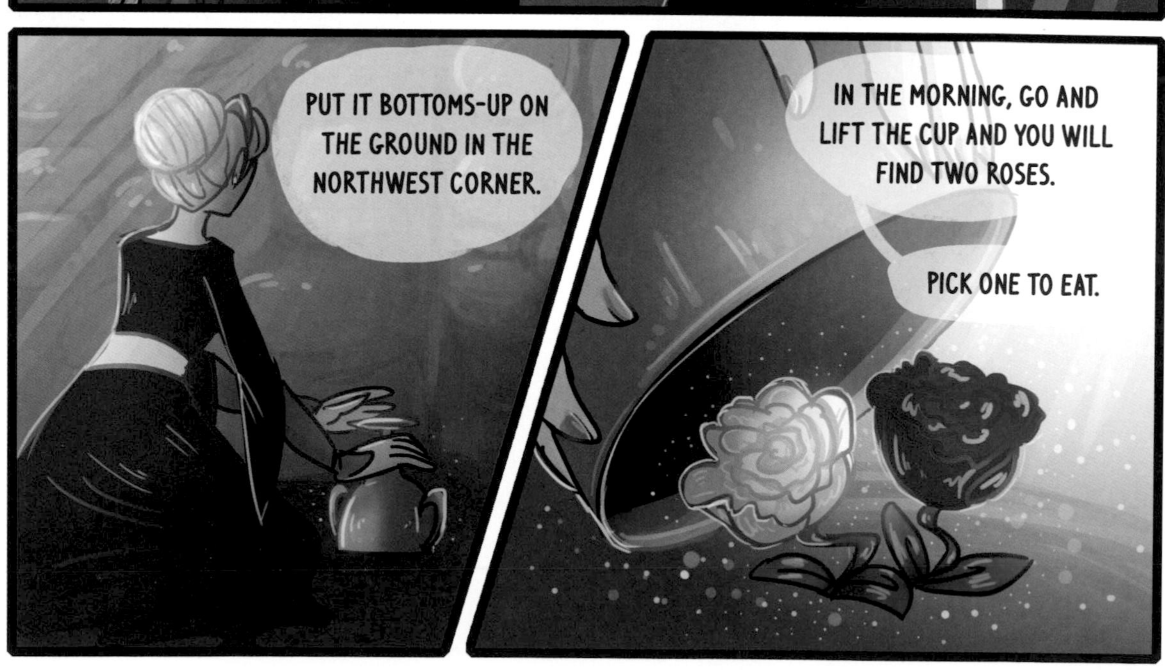
PUT IT BOTTOMS-UP ON THE GROUND IN THE NORTHWEST CORNER.
IN THE MORNING, GO AND LIFT THE CUP AND YOU WILL FIND TWO ROSES.
PICK ONE TO EAT.

IF YOU EAT THE WHITE ROSE, A LITTLE GIRL WILL BE BORN.
IF YOU PICK THE RED ROSE, YOU WILL HAVE A LITTLE BOY.
BUT I WARN YOU, DO NOT EAT BOTH!
IF YOU EAT BOTH THE ROSES, TERRIBLE EVENTS SHALL OCCUR.
REMEMBER: ONLY ONE!
AFTER THINKING HARD ABOUT IT, THE QUEEN FINALLY CHOSE TO EAT THE WHITE ROSE.
BUT IT TASTED TOO SWEET AND DELICIOUS. SHE COMPLETELY FORGOT THE WITCH'S WARNING AND ATE THE RED ROSE AS WELL.
NINE MONTHS LATER, WHEN THE KING WAS AWAY...
AAAAAAAAA
TWINS WERE BORN. THE YOUNGER WAS A HEALTHY, ROSY BABY BOY. BUT BEFORE HE ARRIVED...

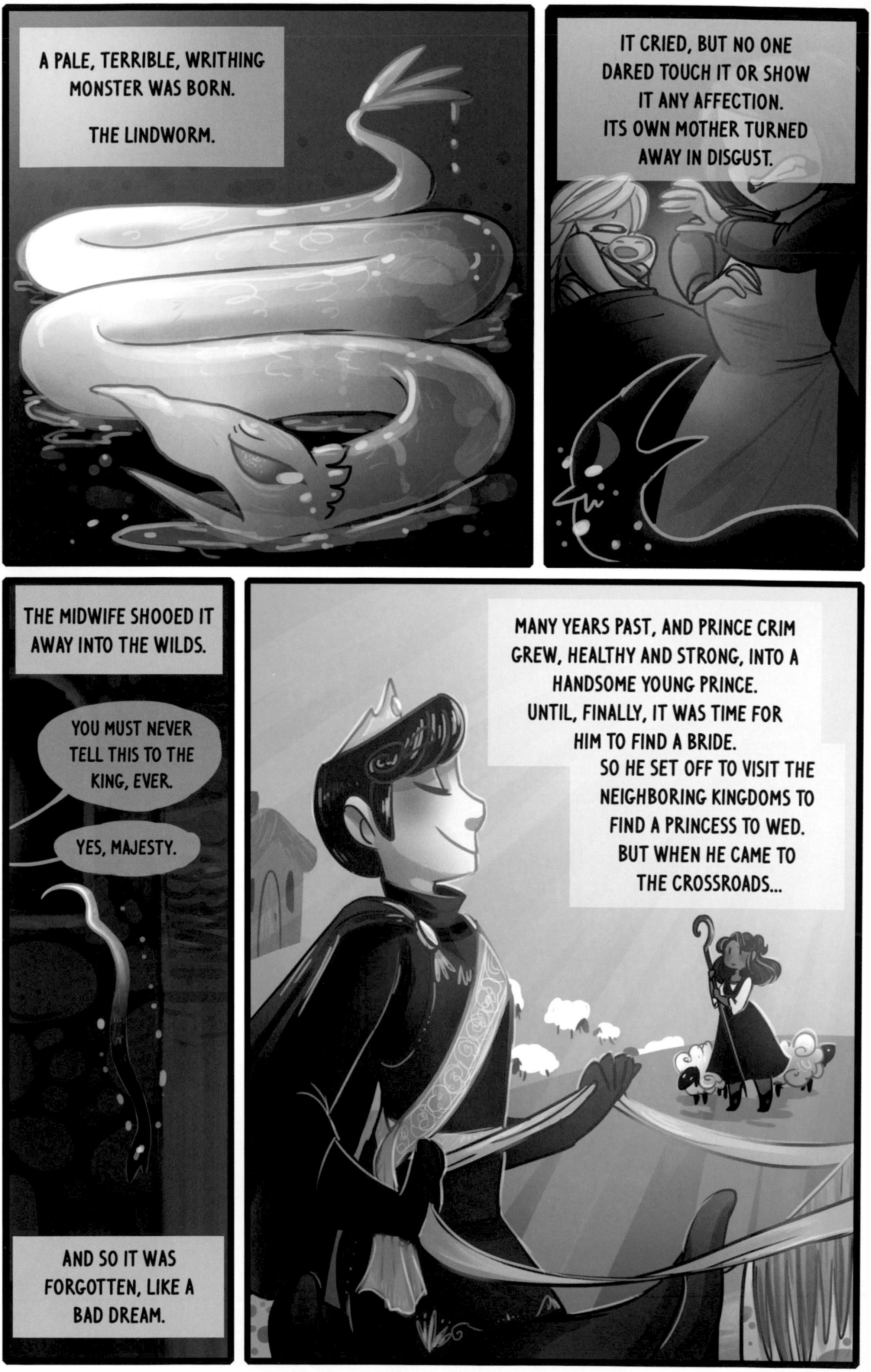

MANY YEARS PAST, AND PRINCE CRIM GREW, HEALTHY AND STRONG, INTO A HANDSOME YOUNG PRINCE. UNTIL, FINALLY, IT WAS TIME FOR HIM TO FIND A BRIDE.

SO HE SET OFF TO VISIT THE NEIGHBORING KINGDOMS TO FIND A PRINCESS TO WED. BUT WHEN HE CAME TO THE CROSSROADS...

THE LINDWORM WAS WAITING.
IT BLOCKED EVERY PATH THE PRINCE TRIED, AND ONLY OPENED ITS MAW TO SAY:
A BRIDE FOR ME BEFORE A BRIDE FOR YOU
THE PRINCE WENT HOME WITH THE STORY AND HIS MOTHER TEARFULLY CONFESSED EVERYTHING.
THAT YES, THE LINDWORM WAS TRULY HIS OLDER SIBLING, AND BY RIGHT MUST BE WED BEFORE CRIM COULD DO SO.

TWICE THE KING WROTE TO THE NEIGHBORING KINGDOMS TO SEND PRINCESSES TO MARRY HIS CHILD (HE DIDN'T SPECIFY WHICH ONE)...
TWICE THERE WAS A GRAND WEDDING...
AND TWICE THE PRINCESSES WERE DEVOURED DURING THEIR WEDDING NIGHTS.
AND YET THE BEAST STILL REPEATED THE SAME PHRASE:
A BRIDE FOR ME BEFORE A BRIDE FOR YOU
FINALLY, IN A FIT OF DESPERATION, THE KING SOUGHT THE HELP OF THE ROYAL SHEPHERD, A MAN WHO LIVED WITH HIS ONLY DAUGHTER.

PLEASE, MY FRIEND, I NEED YOUR DAUGHTER TO MARRY MY CHILD, THE LINDWORM.

SIRE, SHE'S MY ONLY DAUGHTER. I CANNOT GIVE HER UP. SHE'S KIND AND GENTLE AND MUCH TOO GOOD FOR SUCH A TERRIBLE FATE. PLEASE.

BUT THE KING PERSISTED, AND EVENTUALLY THE SHEPHERD AGREED TO HAVE HIS DAUGHTER WED THE BEAST.

...KARI?
YES, FATHER?

!!!

YOUNG LADY?

YOU LOOK TROUBLED, MY DEAR. WHAT IS WRONG?
IT'S NO USE, YOU COULDN'T HELP ME EVEN IF I TOLD YOU.
TRY ME,
I MAY SURPRISE YOU.

HOW CAN YOU? I AM TO MARRY THE LINDWORM, WHO HAS EATEN TWO PRINCESSES BEFORE ME!

WHY WOULD IT SPARE A SHEPHERD GIRL LIKE ME?

Pat

DON'T CRY, YOUNG ONE, AND LISTEN CAREFULLY TO THIS...

SO THE WITCH TOLD KARI OF A WAY SHE COULD SAVE HER LIFE ON HER WEDDING NIGHT,
AND SHE LISTENED WELL, FOR HER VERY LIFE WAS ON THE LINE.

THE NEXT DAY, THERE WAS A WEDDING, LIKE THE FIRST TWO. ALTHOUGH IT FELT MORE LIKE A FUNERAL PROCESSION.
BUT BEFORE KARI WENT TO HER WEDDING NIGHT, SHE REQUESTED A FEW ITEMS BE BROUGHT TO HER CHAMBERS.

TEN SNOW WHITE SHIFTS...
A BARREL OF LYE AND A BARREL OF MILK...
LYE
AND SEVERAL WHIPS...
AND THUS THE NEW BRIDE FACED HER DOOM...
MAIDEN, SHED A SHIFT.
LINDWORM, SHED A SKIN.

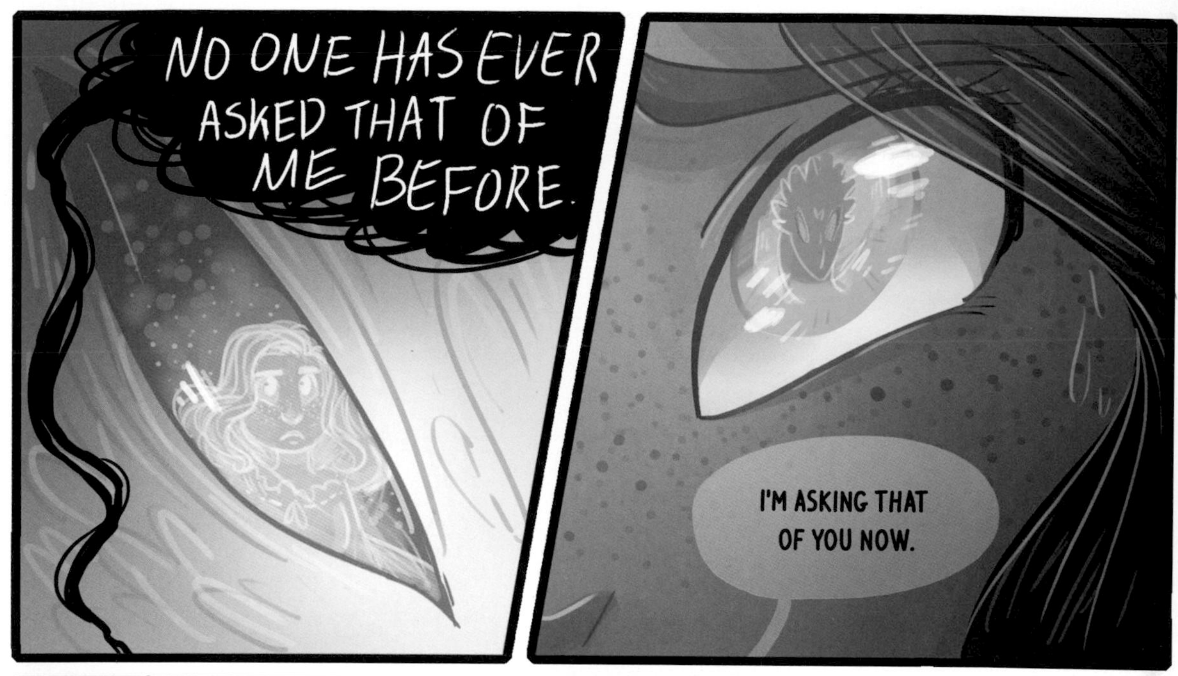

THIS CONTINUED UNTIL SHED SKINS AND SHED SHIFTS LITTERED THE FLOOR.

UNTIL KARI WAS DOWN TO HER FINAL SHIFT...

MAIDEN...

GRAB!!

LYE

DIP!!

AAAH
MILK
AAAAAH

oof
nnn...

OHH MY HEAD...
GASP!!

SNRK

HAHAHAH

AND SO A GREAT CELEBRATION WAS HELD THROUGHOUT THE KINGDOM,

AND THE NEW PRINCESS ROZA (FORMERLY LINDWORM), AND HER BRAVE BRIDE KARI LIVED HAPPILY EVER AFTER.

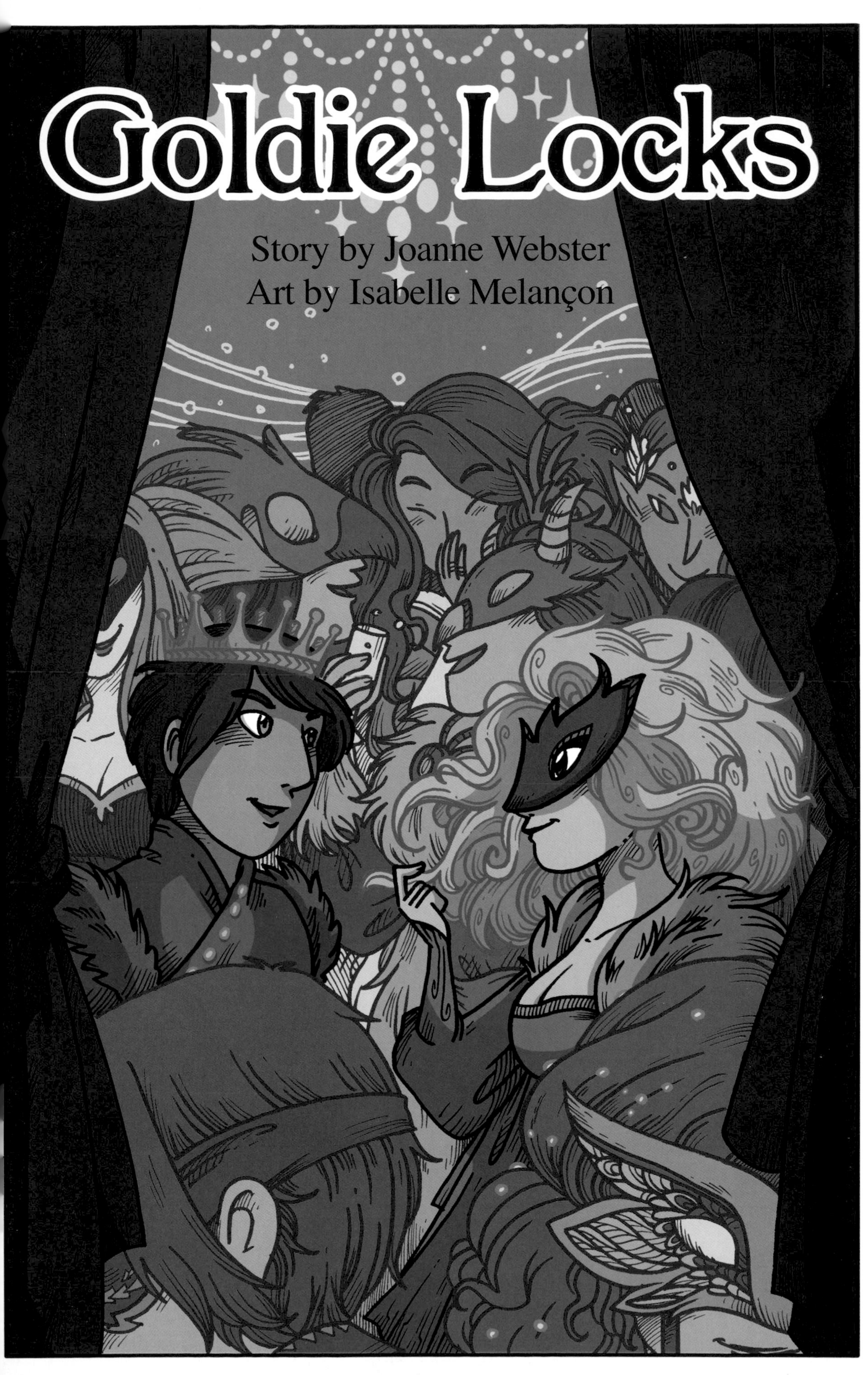

Goldie Locks
Story by Joanne Webster
Art by Isabelle Melançon

Goldie double-checked that her mask was securely on before entering the ballroom. She was grateful Maria managed to convince Lady Marigold to allow Goldie to go in her stead. Getting past the guards was far easier with an official invitation, even if it was rather well known that Lady Marigold would rather spend an evening in a haunted swamp than attend a party at King Bear's castle. Add to the mix that it was a masquerade, and that the guards had been given an "anonymous" gift earlier that evening of a crate of wine, and the result was that no one could be bothered to check who was who under each mask.

The break-in job Maria had given her was off to a splendid start. Saying no to Maria was like saying no to an angel. Maria was the kindest person Goldie knew and she was always glad to take on a job for her. Even if completing the job meant risking her life. King Bear would chop off her head if he knew Goldie was here.

Goldie gazed around the room as she attempted to locate the members of the Royal Bear family. As usual, the royal family would be the only ones wearing their crowns. It was highly discouraged to wear anything crown-like in the King and Queen's presence. Their crowns were their pride and theirs alone to wear. Goldie did think it was silly, but it certainly made it easier to spot them on the dance floor before sneaking into their chambers. Goldie was just thankful the Royal Bear family were humans as it is always harder to steal from elves or trolls, who had heightened sense of hearing and smell. Goldie always felt on edge around them, she swore sometimes they could tell she was a thief by her scent alone. Either way, those abilities made it harder to not be caught red-handed.

She recalled how the Troll Queen pursued her scent into the forest when she made the mistake of wearing her favorite perfume during a job. If Goldie hadn't found that griffon to ride, she would have been caught for sure!

It was admittedly hard to tell, given the elaborate costumes, just who was a real fairy, troll, satyr or elf, and which were simply costumes worn by human nobles. It seemed the Bears had not only invited every human nobleman and noblewoman in the country, but also the ambassadors of the many enchanted neighboring countries. With King Bear assuming they were about to obtain control over Queen Maria's country, he and his Queen probably wagered they had a reason to celebrate.

Goldie had reached the refreshment table when a boisterous laugh echoed in her ears. She turned her head to see a large, brutish man. He was short, but his fists were as big as dinner plates, looking as if they could punch a hole through a tree trunk. His face was decorated by a thick beard and a very simple black mask. A giant, glittering crown sat atop his head, lost in a thick mound of dark and grey-streaked hair, clearly marking him as the Bear King.

He was laughing with one of the elves, his massive hand resting and almost crushing the frail being's shoulder. Now where are his Queen and the Prince? Goldie gazed around and saw the Queen hadn't ventured too far from her husband. She was taller, but her body was as round and plump as the King's. Goldie had heard rumors that the Queen's words were as merciless as the King's anger. The Queen's hands were as huge as the King's. Her hair was a dark brown and had been neatly pulled back into a bun held by several jeweled hair pins. She was off to the sidelines chatting with a couple of noblewomen. Her mask was more elaborate than the King's, and the shimmer of her crown matched her husband's

Goldie surveyed the party looking for the Prince. She felt a light brush against her back and rapidly twirled to lock eyes with her target in question.

As the petticoat of her dress swished around her legs, Goldie quickly looked the prince over and had to admit Maria had been correct. The Prince was attractive, but had a rather small and unimposing frame compared to his parents. His hair was the same thick brown as the king and queen and provided needed padding for his heavy crown to rest, a tad crooked, on top of his head.

"Sorry!" said Prince Robert. Goldie was surprised to see he wasn't wearing a mask. "I wasn't watching where I was going."

Goldie collected herself, startled by both the apology and the fact that he managed to sneak up on her, and curtsied. "It's fine, sire. I'm more than happy to be bumped into if it's by a member of royalty, especially a handsome one." She gave him her best flirty smile. "And even more so if that royal were to offer me a drink."

Prince Robert seemed baffled by her suggestion but gave a light chuckle. "I'll admit, I haven't heard that as a response before."

"May I ask why you aren't wearing a mask?"

Robert gave a half smile as he offered her a glass. "I hardly see the point of concealing my identity when my mother refuses to let me take my crown off. The evening would be much more pleasant without it. For one, the weight seems to be hindering my ability to dance or lean slightly towards guests."

"Ah," Goldie said as she eyed the crown. It would be so tempting to let it slip into her purse. "Doesn't look that heavy."

Robert fingered the crown as his bright green eyes dimmed and he gave a bitter frown. "It feels heavier when you consider the price that comes with it."

Goldie raised an eyebrow at the prince's weighted comment. She pretended to drink absent-mindedly.

"Who might you be?" Robert asked, as he took a tart. "Your voice doesn't sound familiar in the least."

Goldie grinned. "Now, what is the point of a masquerade if I tell you my name? You could guess or wait for the traditional Midnight Unmasking like everyone else."

"I doubt I could guess," Robert said as he pointed to her hair. "I don't know anyone whose hair is as golden and curly as yours."

Goldie proudly twirled a strand of her bright, wavy hair around her finger as she approached him. "Not many people in my country have this hair color, so it makes me unique. I like being unforgettable."

Goldie stepped forward and suddenly fell forward, pretending to trip on the hem of her dress. As she predicted, the gallant Prince swiftly caught her. "Are you alright?" he asked, holding her with both arms as his crown slid lopsided to the right.

"Yes, sorry," Goldie said as she gripped his side, pretending to regain her composure as her fingers discreetly slipped into his coat pocket. With great stealth, she slipped them out while calling attention to her feet. "Such annoying shoes," she said with an adorable pout, "they make my toes pinch."

"I see," Robert said. "Do you need to sit down-"

"Robert!" the King called out. "Come greet the Dwarf King's ambassador!"

Robert gave a tired sigh before he bowed to Goldie. "Excuse me, I'll only be a moment."

Goldie smiled as she watched him go to the King's side. Maria had been right. The Prince didn't seem to carry his father's ambition. He seems out of place in this grand ball. She turned her gaze away from Robert, and looked to the keys she now held. Goldie smiled, she had what she needed, so it was time for phase two. Goldie cautiously left the ballroom, and slipped into the stairway.

According to the castle layout, the royal chambers were a couple of flights up. She grunted as she lifted the various layers of her skirt. From her sources, the King had hidden the spell books in one of the royal bedrooms. Goldie had no choice but to search them all. For that, she needed the prince's keys. The royal chambers were protected by an enchantment. Her trusty skeleton key would not be able to open those doors. She heard guards approaching. She slipped in a nearby closet and listened to the guards footsteps as they passed. Goldie then tore off the gown and bodice to reveal the plain dark tunic and trousers she had been wearing underneath. She replaced the decorative ballroom mask with a simpler black to keep her face hidden. Goldie then adjusted the belt wrapped around her waist to ensure that both her pouch and her knife holster were set.

"Much better," Goldie muttered as she tucked the glittering, charmed keys into her pouch. Goldie spotted the royal emblem crowning a large wooden door. She knew it had to be King Bear's chambers. She plucked the heaviest of her magical keys and inserted it into the old iron lock. She gave a joyous grin as a soft click echoed as it turned. A shine appeared over the door and vanished, which was a signal that the spell that had been keeping her out was broken. The room was hers for the taking now. Goldie entered and cast her gaze about the room. It was exactly as she had expected. The walls were covered top to bottom in the animal skins and mounted heads of King Bear's hunting prizes. Among the beastly decor he had hung several flattering ornate portraits of himself.

The drawers, bed canopy and even the mirrors were gold encrusted and had jewels sticking out of them like a jagged cave wall. Goldie was tempted to snag a jewel or two, but she was racing against the clock. Midnight was approaching. She began her search.

Goldie's blood boiled at the thought of King Bear as she rummaged through his belongings. Not only had he secretly stolen Maria's spellbook, but he was demanding that Maria cede the throne to him if she wished to keep her people safe from the rampage of the dragons. It was hard to believe those old spellbooks were the only thing keeping the nightmarish monsters out of her country. Goldie remembered the history lessons in school about how difficult it was to live under the constant threat of the dragons. The number of children eaten per year was particularly horrifying. Despite that, she wasn't sure which was the worst beast for her country to deal with, the dragons or King Bear. Maria wasn't ready to test if her country could survive without the spellbook. Hence why she had called her childhood friend, an expert thief, to her aid. Goldie would be declared a national hero for generations to come. She liked the idea, maybe they would even write a song or name a holiday after her.

Goldie checked every hiding spot she could think of, every drawer, closet and conceivable hidden compartment. She even lifted the mattress and checked underneath, but besides discovering the King slept on a bed that was as hard as a rock, she found no hint of the spellbook.

The Queen's chambers were next on the list. No hunting trophies on her walls, but there were just as many portraits as the king's room had heads. The portraits were encircled by layers of lace and velvet. In any spot where lace and velvet weren't found sat giant, ugly vases filled with blood-red roses. None of this ornamentation, however, topped the gaudy miniature gold statue depicting the Queen herself sitting next to the vanity table.

"Nice to see the country's tax money is spent wisely," Goldie muttered, as she flicked the statue's forehead and continued her search.

Once again, she searched through the closet, drawers, tapped the walls and every other imaginable hiding spot. Besides discovering the the Queen's bed was far too soft for her liking, her search yielded the same results as the King's room.

The spellbook wasn't here.

The spellbook had to be in Prince Robert's room, it was the only logical conclusion. She glanced at the clock and saw she had less than an hour left before the guests would be removing their masks.

She found Robert's room. Goldie noted the Prince's room was unembellished in comparison to his parents' rooms. The bed had a simple design. Or at least as simple as a bed for royalty could be. There were gorgeous paintings of rivers and valleys, and a detailed map of the world hung on the far wall. There was no gold or jewelry in sight.

She didn't know why she was glad to discover he was more practical, and Goldie didn't have time to decipher why she cared. Just as in the previous rooms, Goldie was thorough. She searched the drawers, closet and every trunk in the room. Desperate, she let out a curse as she sat in the large chair. Where on earth could they have hidden it?

She drummed her fingers on the armchair's cushion. The book was large, so it had to be hidden in something fairly noticeable. Goldie leaned back. The back of the chair was oddly lumpy.

The King's chair had been as hard as a slab of stone, while the Queen's had been too soft; Goldie had been certain she would be sucked in, and never seen again. But no, the Prince's chair was just right, except for that odd spot directly in the middle of her back.

Goldie stood up and traced her fingers over where the cushion felt hard. She grinned as she realized her fingers were moving in a rectangular shape.

Goldie drew the knife from her holster and sliced the edge of the panel to easily slip her hand inside. She held back gleeful laughter as she removed the fabric, unveiling an old book with a cover engraved with ancient lettering.

"Found it," Goldie said as she held up the book. "This was too easy."

"I agree."

Goldie spun around, clutching the book to her chest. A blow knocked her knife away. She protectively held onto the book as Robert kicked the knife under his bed and turned to her with a frown.

"I thought I might find you here," he said as his eyes narrowed. "When I couldn't find you at the party."

"You looked for me, did you?" Goldie said with a small grin, doing her best to hide the sudden dread that she had been caught. He was suspicious from the start? She really needed to work on her disguises more.

"Yes, because it's midnight," Robert said as he approached her. "So, it's time to remove your mask."

Goldie tried to dodge, but the Prince was surprisingly fast and ripped her mask away. She narrowed her eyes as Robert stepped back and looked her over. "I know you," he said. "I saw your wanted poster back when I was staying in the Eastern Islands last summer."

"Oh?" Goldie said. "And who am I?"

"Goldie Locks," Robert said as he twirled her mask in his hands. "The famous thief, rumoured to be the adoptive sister to Queen Maria."

"You forgot THE most beautiful maiden in the land," Goldie said with a laugh. "I won't deny being a thief, but," she gave a shrug. "I assure you, that the rumour about the Queen is false. I'm hardly that important. "

"If it is," Robert said as he pointed to the book in hand. "Why did you sneak in here to steal that book? It would hold little value to anyone other than her."

Goldie raised a finger. "To sell it back to the queen perhaps? Or to your father? Stealing something stolen is hardly stealing. It's more like distributing the wealth." she dropped her smile, and stared accusingly at Robert. "After all, wealth is what you expected to gain when your family stole it from Queen Maria. To force her to hand her country over to you on a silver platter."

Robert went quiet, his hands tightened into fists. "That has nothing to do with me, that was my father." He looked up solemnly. "I told him it's vile to take over a country like that."

"And yet, you did nothing to stop him." She narrowed her eyes. "Words are meaningless if there's no action to go with them." Oh, that was good! She should save that for a book someday.

Robert seemed hesitant as he stared at the book. "I don't agree with what my father is doing."

"Then why was the book hidden in your room?" Goldie said as she pointed to the chair.

Robert looked down. "I took it. I was hoping to conceal for a while. Talk some sense into him. To change his mind... " He removed his crown and let it roll on his bed.

Goldie frowned. Robert didn't seem to be lying. "Perhaps you were tired of waiting for your kingdom and thought you'd use the spells in the book to claim both Queen Maria's and the Bear kingdom as your own?"

Robert's eyes widened. "Is that what you think of me!" he shouted. "I hate this," he muttered.

"Then don't stop me," Goldie replied sharply as she pointed to the window behind him that she had hoped to use to escape. It would be too risky to go back the way she came with the book in her hands. "Walk away, and pretend you didn't see me."

"I can't," Robert replied as Goldie drew closer to him. "I don't agree with my father, but I can't betray him."

Goldie gave him a sincere smile. The guy was loyal, the same way she was to Maria, and she couldn't deny it was an admirable trait. "Don't worry," she said as she reached inside her pouch and brought out a tiny sack filled with powder. "You wouldn't be betraying anyone if you suddenly went to sleep."

Robert scoffed. "I'm hardly going to go to sleep-"

Goldie flung the sack towards his chest. It broke on impact, flooding his lungs with sleeping powder. Robert coughed uncontrollably and leaned on the bed. His crown dropped to the floor. Robert staggered, unable to stay conscious, and landed on the floor next to the crown. Once quiet snores could be heard, Goldie rose and walked towards the window. "And I was hoping to not have to buy more of Rose's sleeping powder when I got back."

Standing in the window frame, she looked back at the slumbering Prince. She brushed her curls out of her eyes and grunted.

"I'm getting soft." Goldie walked back to the prince and flopped him onto his bed. Why did the Prince have to be so heavy? "There, at least you're off the floor." She laughed as she felt the mattress. "Glad to see you have better taste in beds than your parents." She stared at his sleeping face for a moment before placing her mask in his hands.

Goldie headed to the window and blew a kiss to the sleeping prince. "See you around, Robert! Got to admit, I do like you, but that's my secret," she admitted before climbing out the window.

Queen Maria thanked her maid for serving the tea, and then turned her attention back to Goldie. "So, how did you get out? Winged shoes? Enchanted beanstalks?"

"Just the usual, used my grappling hook, and climbed down the castle wall," Goldie shrugged as she stuffed a scone into her mouth. "Then while the guards were busy getting drunk, thanks to the wine I bribed them with, found a horse that was in desperate need of liberation, and was out of there before anyone noticed."

Maria fiddled her hands nervously. "And where's the book?"

Goldie smirked as she revealed the book she'd been keeping behind her back. "Here! An early birthday present."

Maria sighed with relief as she took the book, and flipped through the pages. "Goldie, I'm in your debt."

"You're darn right," Goldie said as she hung her legs over the chair arm, and sipped her tea. "You have no idea what a pain in the butt it was to get it back."

Maria only laughed, as she set the book on the table. "And how should I pay you?"

Goldie traced her finger over the brim of her cup. Normally, a job like this would be double her rate, but it was Maria. "Nothing."

Maria rolled her eyes. "Goldie, if you think you're getting away without me properly thanking you, forget it."

Goldie sighed. "Fine, give me a bag of gold, a three-layer chocolate cake, a national holiday and we're even."

"With tea, I'm assuming?"

Goldie snorted. "Of course with tea, it'd be barbaric to have cake and no tea."

Maria chuckled as she folded her hands into her lap. "And you're certain only Prince Robert saw you?"

Goldie nodded, grimly. "Yeah, so I'm betting we'll be getting an angry letter from King Bear

demanding you hand me over when the Prince tells him."

"I don't believe that will be a problem," Maria said as she leaned forward as a mischievous smirk appeared. "Funny thing, I did recieve a couple of letters, but not from King Bear."

Goldie sat up straight as Maria brought out two letters from her skirt pocket. "They are both from Prince Robert," Maria explained. "The first one is addressed to me. He humbly apologizes for what his father has done, and has asked if he may come personally to make amends. Also, apparently he kept the fact that he saw you steal the book a secret."

Goldie scoffed. "He's probably doing that to cover his butt, so you don't decide to declare war on them for stealing your book."

"Perhaps," Maria replied, and handed the second letter over. "However, this one is addressed to you, my dear."

Goldie choked on her tea, as she took the letter, and broke the seal.

Dear Goldie,

I wanted you to know that I will no longer let my parents dictate my life. I'm going to start to act like a proper ruler to my country. I'm working with my council, and with the citizens to officially and properly take the crown away from my father. It will take time, but thankfully both my people and the council have had enough with my father's selfish actions.

Some time in the future, I will be coming to your homeland to make amends to Queen Maria and would like to get you know you better.

Sincerely, Prince Robert

P.S. I was half awake when you blew me that kiss.

Goldie's jaw dropped. *The little sneak saw that?!*

"Well," Maria said. "What does it say?"

Goldie tried desperately to hide her blush and folded the letter. "It's nothing."

"You are lying," Maria said as she swiped the letter back.

"Hey! That's private correspondence!"

"I am the Queen, I get my way," Maria said as she stuck out her tongue before her eyes skimmed the letter, grinning. "Oh my." She laughed. "It looks like he was quite taken by you."

Goldie sighed as she sipped her tea. "I can't see why? I knocked him out and stole the book under his nose."

Maria leaned back in her chair. "You don't realize it, Goldie, but your words have a powerful effect on people."

Goldie gave her friend a little smile. Perhaps she would attempt to steal his heart next. And this time, he would not be able to catch her doing it.

Masks

Story & Art by Megan Kearney

NO GONDOLAS COME OR GO AFTER SUNSET.
I UNDERSTAND.

SPOOKY PLACE... NOTHING LEFT NOW BUT ANIMALS AN' GHOSTS.

TP
LISTEN, I DUNNO WHY YOU WANNA COME TO A PLACE LIKE THIS, HONEY.
YOU'RE A NICE GIRL--

...AM I?

...
TP
TP
TP
TP

MM, SUCH LOVELY HAIR.

...AND SUCH A CLEVER GIRLTO FIND A GONDOLEER WILLING TO COME HERE SO CLOSE TO SUNSET.

...WILL YOU JOIN THE MASQUE?

... CLEVER I MAY BE, BUT NO VIXEN AM I.
WE ALL JOIN EVENTUALLY, MY DEAR!
BETTER TO CHOOSE THE MASK YOURSELF!
TROMP TROMP
VWIP
FWIP

OH!

AH!
SHE'S NIMBLE!
QUICK, SHE IS!
A GOOD CATCH, SHE'S FAST!

LADY, WILL YOU JOIN THE MASQUE?

...FAST I MAY BE, BUT NO SQUIRREL AM I.

...TOO QUICK TO DISAGREE, SHE IS.

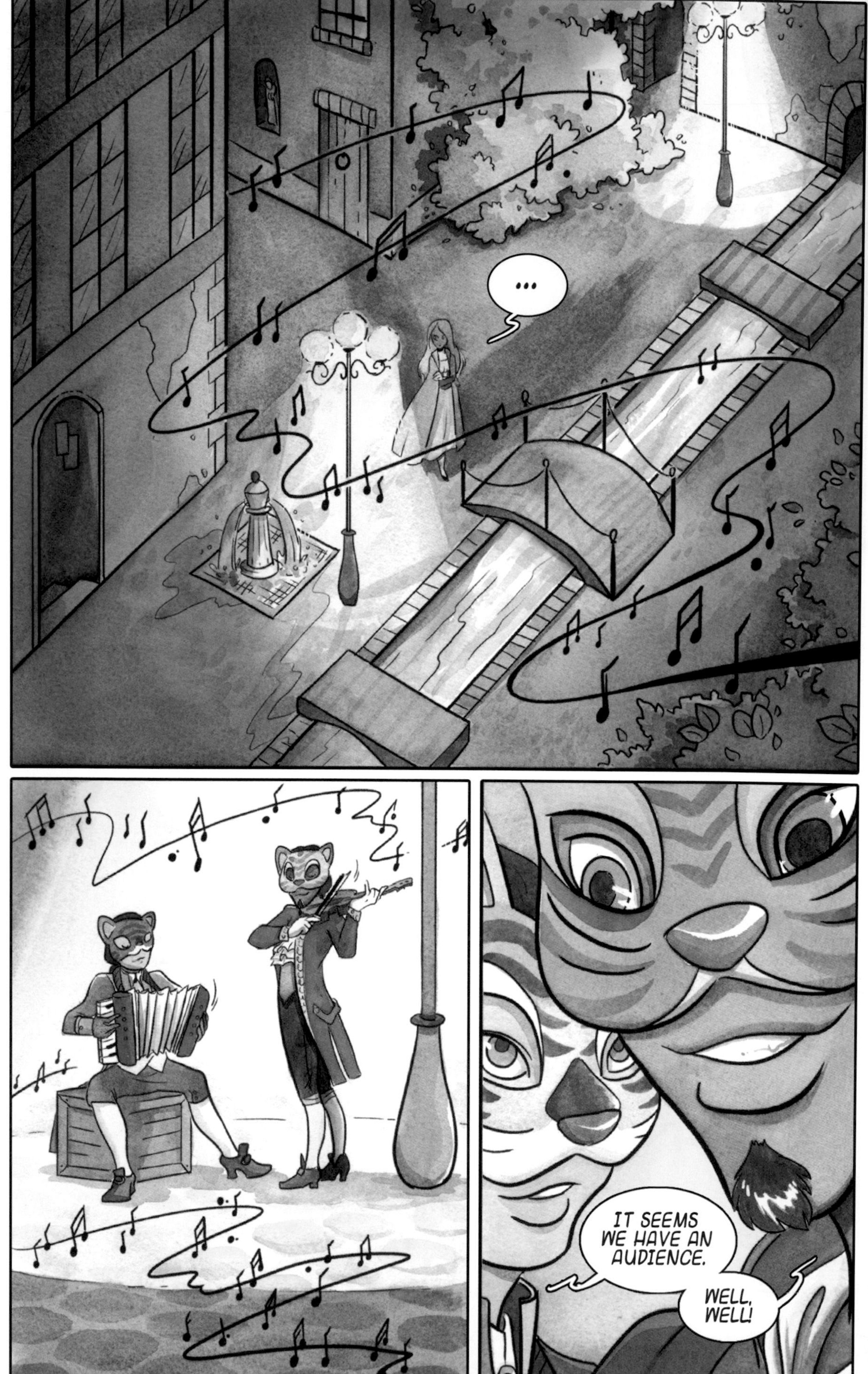
...
IT SEEMS WE HAVE AN AUDIENCE.
WELL, WELL!

I--
I'M NOT--
WHERE ARE YOU OFF TO, LOVE? YOU WOULDN'T LEAVE US WITHOUT A DANCE, WOULD YOU?
COME NOW, DON'T BE RUDE! GIVE US A SMILE!

I--
SHE'S A PRETTY ONE, ISN'T SHE?
WHAT'S WRONG, PET? CAT GOT YOUR TONGUE?

SO, WILL YOU JOIN THE MASQUE, THEN, KITTEN?
SHE'D MAKE A PRETTY PUSS, I WAGER--QUIET AS A CAT.

HAHAHAHAHAHA
OH, DON'T RUN OFF NOW, SWEETHEART!
STAY AND PLAY A TUNE WITH US!
!
TP TP TP TP TP TP TP TP TP

HAHH
HAHH
TP
TP
TP
AH!
WELL, WELL!
WHUMP
OH, MY!
WAIT, GIRL--
--MAKE A CHOICE--
OVER HERE, HONEY--
HERE--
--SWEET HEART--
LADY--
NO, WE WANT HER--
JOIN THE MASQUE--
--WE ALL JOIN IN THE END--
COME BACK--!
GIRL!
TP TP TP TP
HUP
--DON'T RUN--
--HEY, SWEETIE--
HEY, GIRL--
COME, JOIN THE MASQUE!

SKTCH
SKTCH

TP TP
TP

HAHH *HAHH*

?

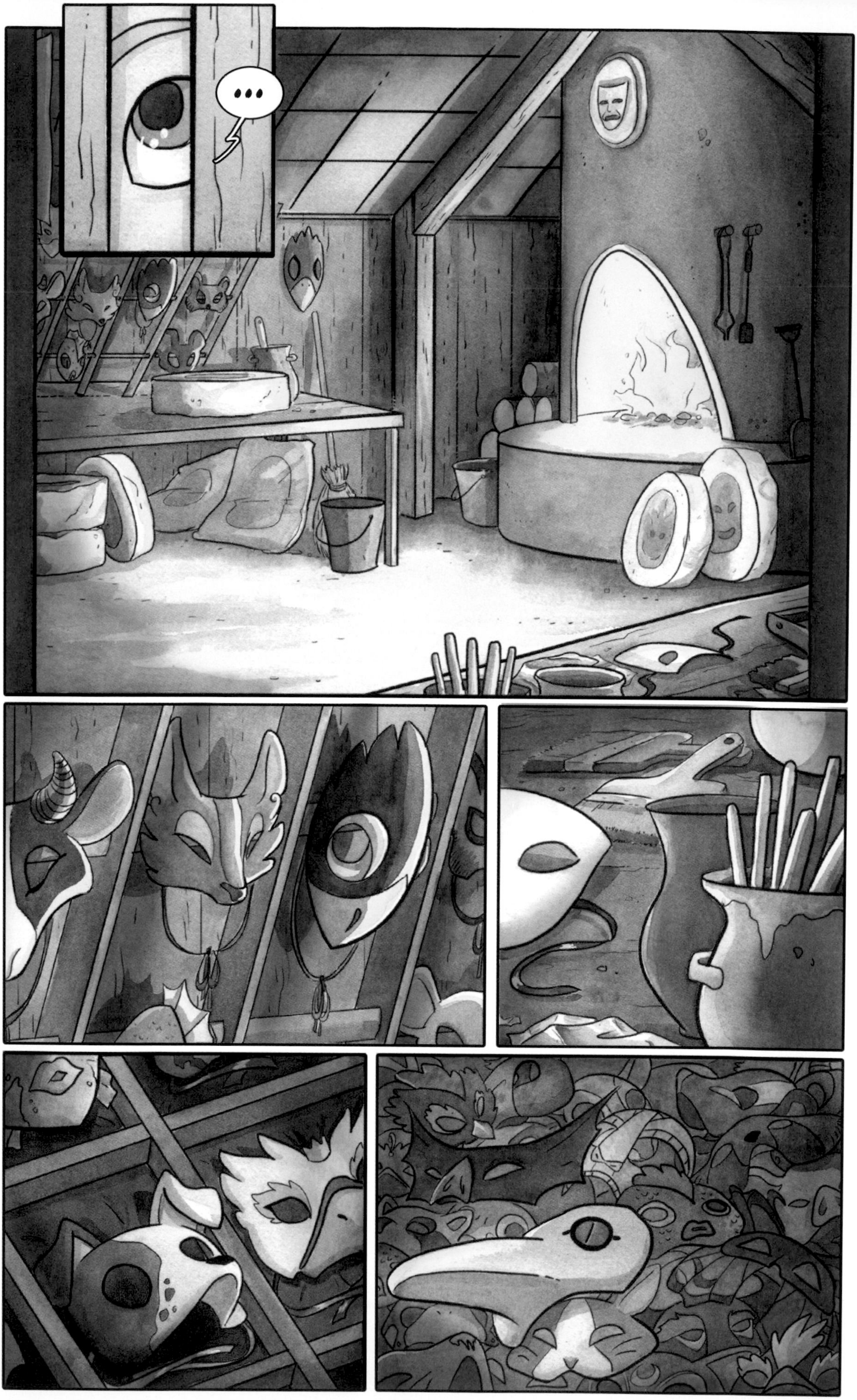

...

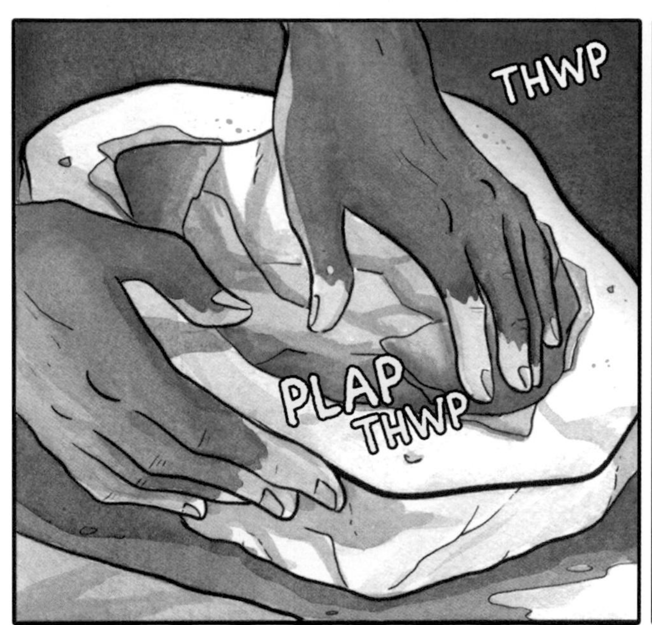

UM... HELLO?

...
...
...YOU'VE DONE WELL TO COME SO FAR.
IT TAKES BRAVERY AND CUNNING TO GO SO LONG WITHOUT HIDING YOUR TRUE FACE...
FEW MAKE IT TO THE ISLAND, MUCH LESS THE WORKSHOP.
...BUT LIFE IS A MASQUERADE.
WE WEAR MASKS EVERY DAY. SOME ARE MORE HONEST THAN OTHERS.
SHFF

...AND REGARDLESS WHETHER IT'S CHOSEN BY ANOTHER, OR OF OUR OWN MAKING...
...IN THE END, WE ALL WEAR A MASK.
...
SO...
NEITHER FOX, NOR FELINE
NOR FOWL OR FISH, NOR FILLY...
... LADY, WILL YOU JOIN THE MASQUE?

...
...
...
CHK

End

Godfather Death

LAURA NEUBERT

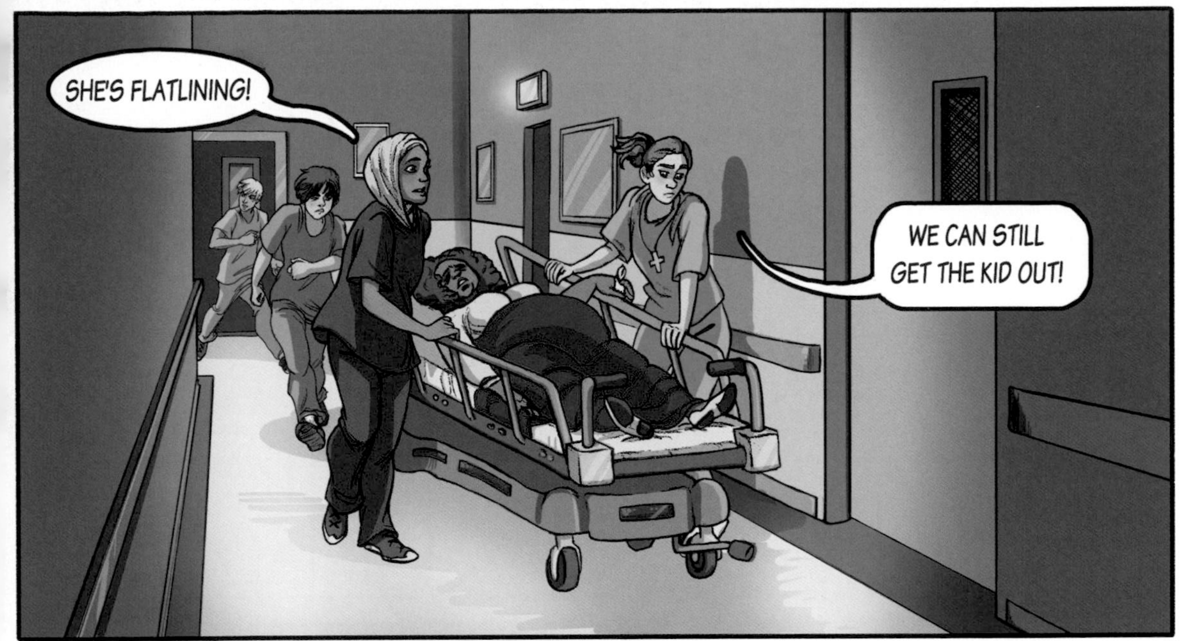
SHE'S FLATLINING!
WE CAN STILL GET THE KID OUT!

LOOKS LIKE MOM'S A JANE DOE.
MAKES THE KID A BABY JANE, RIGHT?

NOT THIS ONE!
SHE EVADED DEATH!

SHE'S A KHALIDA!
HEH, HEH!
MAYBE DEATH CAN BE HER GODPARENT!

ONE MUST SPEAK CAUTIOUSLY OF DEATH.
SOMETIMES I LISTEN...
SOMETIMES I LIKE YOUR IDEAS...

I GAVE MY GODDAUGHTER LITTLE.
WHAT SHE HAD, SHE WORKED FOR.

BUT I DID GRANT HER ONE POWERFUL GIFT.
TO KNOW WITH A GLANCE HOW MUCH LIFE A SOUL HAD LEFT.

DO YOU THINK I'LL MAKE IT TO KEN'S WEDDING, DR. ROSSI?
AH SUGAR, YOU'RE GOING TO OUTLIVE ME!

I'M CONCERNED FOR HIS COMFORT.
LET'S CONSIDER ENDING THE SURGERIES.

YOU JUST PRESS THE ROOF, AND TAD-AH!
IT WEIGHED HEAVILY ON HER, TO KNOW THAT I WAS COMING AND COULD NOT BE STOPPED.

SHE TOLD NO ONE.
BUT OTHERS SENSED IT.

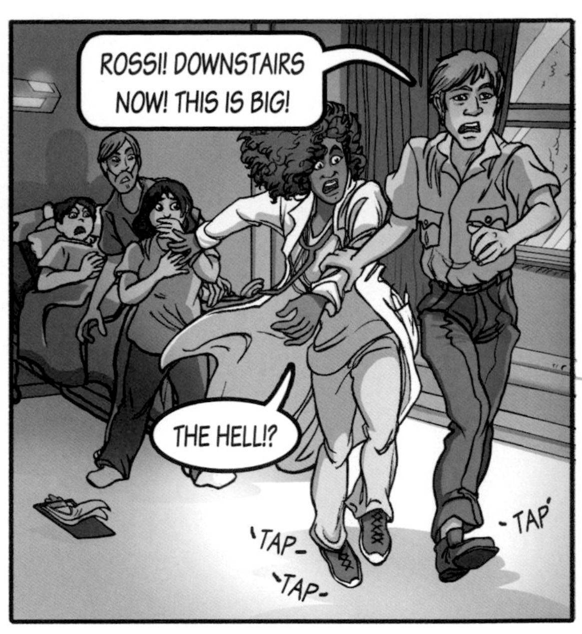
ROSSI! DOWNSTAIRS
NOW! THIS IS BIG!
THE HELL!?
TAP
TAP
TAP

IT'S OUR
BIGGEST DONOR.
BAD, BAD
WRECK.
IF HE GOES, THE
BUDGET IS SHOT.
...CAN'T YOU JUST
DO WHATEVER IT
IS YOU DO?

WE JUST WRAPPED
ON SURGERY.

IS HE GOING TO
BE ALL RIGHT?

HE WILL BE, IF
I CAN HELP IT.

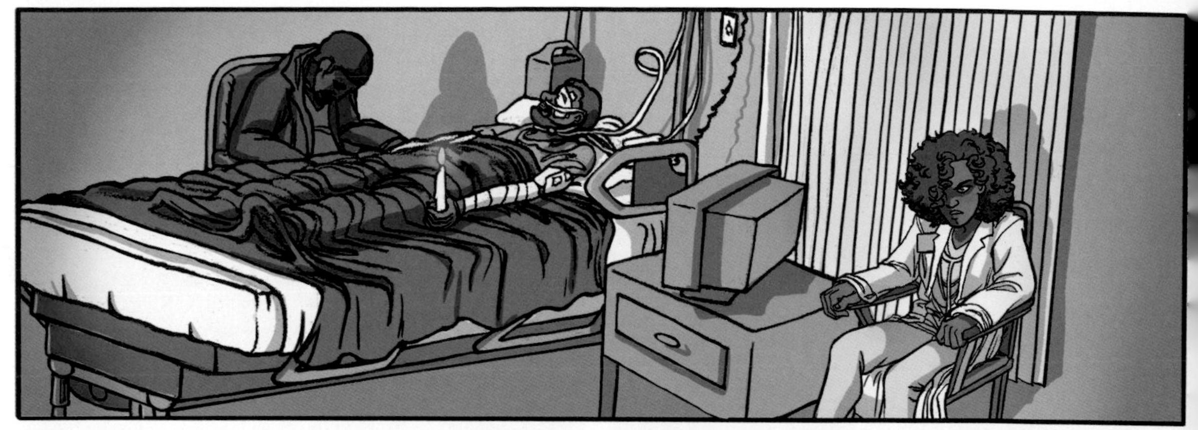

Shhhhh

DAD!
COUGH, COUGH
GASP! COUGH!

OH GOD! I THOUGHT
YOU WERE DEAD!
AVERY...

ONE WEEK LATER.
EXCUSE ME, MISS.
I'M HERE FOR DAD AND MAYBE THIS IS FORWARD, BUT...
DO YOU HAVE A NUMBER?
I'VE GOT THAT AND AN OPEN EVENING.

"THUMP"

WHAT ARE YOU DOING HERE?!

YOU MISUSED MY GIFT, KHALIDA.
I DO NOT LIKE TO BE TRICKED.

HE'S AN IMPORTANT MAN! WITHOUT HIM-
IT'S IRRELEVANT! IT WAS HIS TIME!

SO I WILL GRANT YOU PARDON THIS ONCE...
YOU ARE MY GODCHILD.

BUT KNOW THAT I DO THIS FOR YOU ALONE, KHALIDA.

FOR YOU ALONE...

WHAT'S THE FROWN FOR?
I JUST NEED A BREAK.

WELL, BE PREPARED.
"CLICK"
MOM'S DYING TO MEET YOU.

LET'S NOT TALK ABOUT DEATH, AVERY.
OK...SURE, NO DEATH.

MOM SAID "MAKE SURE SHE GETS HERE HUNGRY!"
HA! SHE'S JUST EXCITED TO SEE A GIRL!

CLANG
OH GOD!
AVERY!
VRRRRREEEEEE

huff,
huff,
huff

KHALIDA!
NOT HIM! ANYONE BUT HIM!

ANYONE?

FWOOOOOSSHHHH

SHHH

BEFORE YOU ARE THE FLAMES OF ALL THOSE LIVING NOW.

SO, WHO SHALL TAKE THE PLACE OF THAT YOUNG MAN?

WHERE IS MY FLAME?

KHALIDA.
I WISHED ONLY
TO SHOW YOU
YOUR FOLLY.

WHERE
IS IT!?

IT IS NOT IN MY
NATURE TO LEAVE SIGNS
BEHIND FOR THE LIVING.

THEY SELDOM
UNDERSTAND.

BUT...
SOMETIMES...

LITTLE FOOLERY
PRESENTS

CRANE WIFE

SCRIPT
Alex Singer

ART
Jayd Ait-Kaci

TYPE
Ariana Maher

When the Master died, I came to the Yamagata household.
The family was very rich, so there were many mourners at the estate.

The family asked me to interview one in particular:

One Lady Mitsuru.

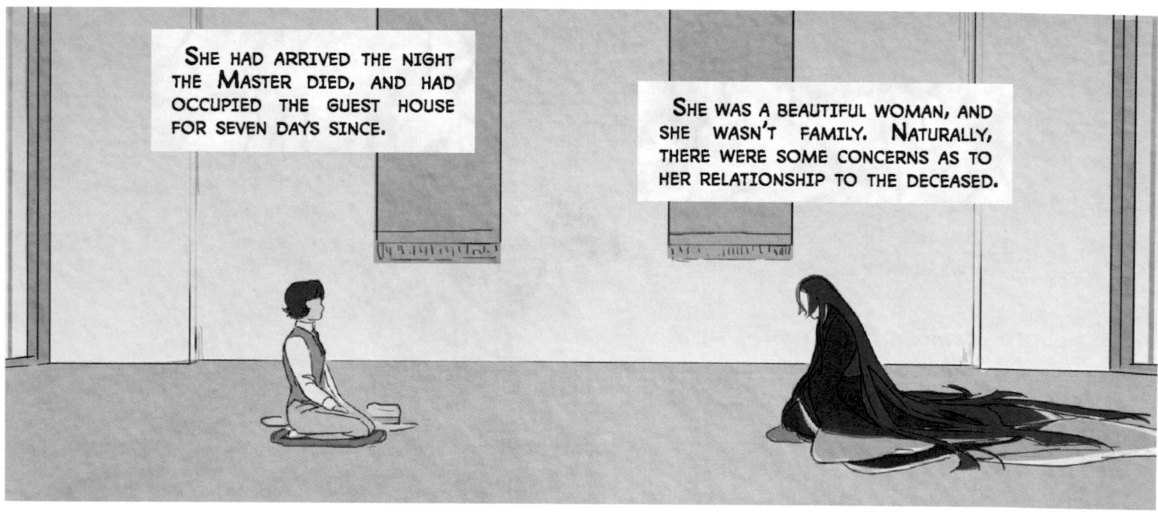
She had arrived the night the Master died, and had occupied the guest house for seven days since.
She was a beautiful woman, and she wasn't family. Naturally, there were some concerns as to her relationship to the deceased.

It seemed silly to dance around the issue, so, as we sat together, I asked...
We met on a cold day in winter.

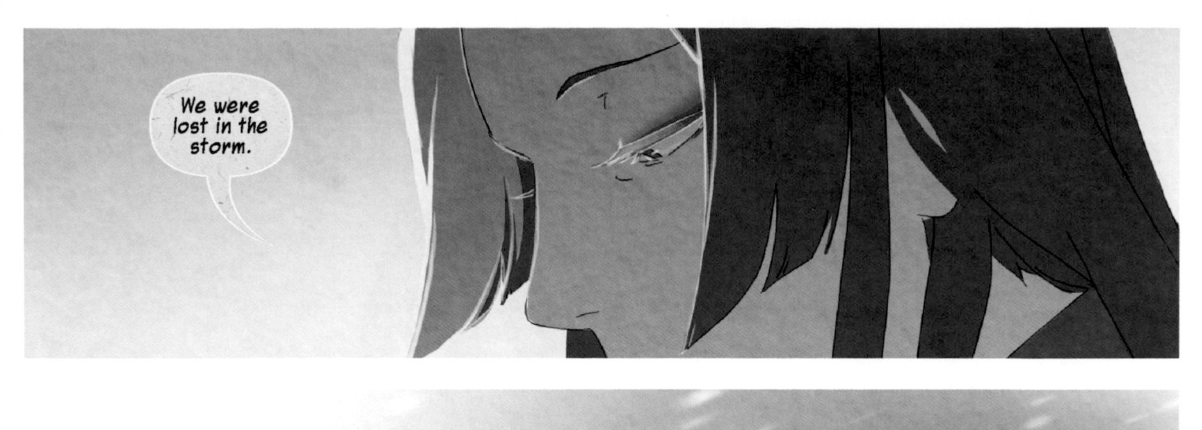

It was a terrible blizzard, and there was blood, so much blood...

We helped one another find our way home.
The hunter's hands were warm. They held me, desperate for life.
When the storm passed, we both went our separate ways.
We were predator and prey, after all.
But we promised that we would do one another a favor.
Though we were poor then, some day our fortunes would change.
In a year's time, I came to keep that promise.

We stayed friends for many years. The family was kind to me.
The master was ruthless, and ambitious.
It mattered to me very much that he do well for himself.
I gave him the means to achieve that ambition,
and the family prospered for many years.

Then there came a time when I was no longer welcome.
The wife grew jealous. I fled to the city.

And was the Master's life... something that you might have taken back, when they asked you to leave?

...Oh.

Ah. Is *that* why they sent you? My, this is embarrassing.

No, of course not. Why would I take back what was given as a gift?

How rude.

No, no. I was promised something quite different than that!

You see, I liked paper cranes.
All those perfect little birds.
Thousands and thousands.
Folded neatly.
Folded perfectly.
On colored paper.
For thirteen years.
After the family sent me away, you see.
The day that they stopped coming, was the day the man died.
They were all quite beautiful.

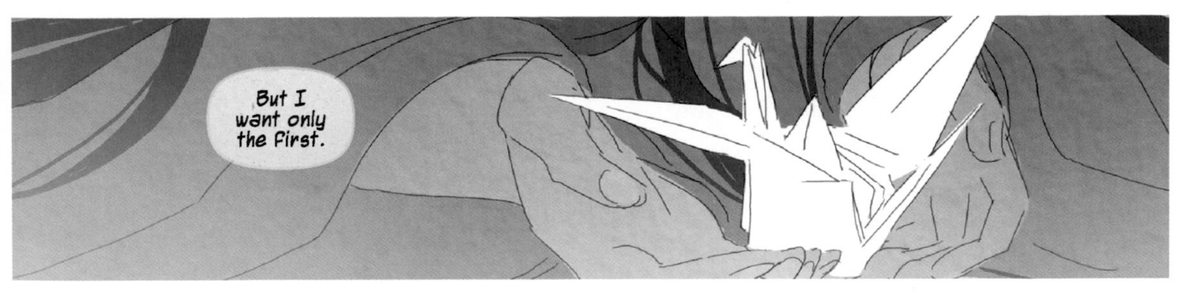
But I want only the first.

It was plain and white, but...
Ah, it was my favorite.
It is still in this house. Once I have that, I shall be on my way...

So that the Yamagata family will know that I did not forget.

...And after that, we finished our tea and said goodbye.
So, you see, it is not as you suspected.
It is *exactly* as I suspected!
I knew that woman was more than she seemed.

I'd known from the day she first came to our house.
So tell me, what do you think she is?
A demon?
A ghoul?

...I think she is only a bird, at one point lost in a storm.
You have nothing to fear from her, so long as you just let her leave as she wishes.
She will take what was owed and leave what was given.

'As she wishes.'
Hmph.
That's brazen.

And all that talk of friendship...
Don't suppose she told you she was my husband's mistress?
That he had me send her money while she was in the city, along with those blasted cranes?

...I didn't have to ask, Lady Yamagata.
Those sorts of stories are not so uncommon.

Ack. You **are** one of those 'modern' women aren't you?

Well, nevermind that.
She will leave us be if we let her go?
Fine!
We're happy to be done with her.

I imagine the feeling is quite mutual.

Thank you for your consultation, Detective.

Tch.

I will have a man see you out.

I LEFT IT AT THAT.
I DIDN'T WANT TO LINGER IN THE YAMAGATA HOUSE, AND NEITHER DID THE CRANE.
I SET UP WARDS, AND TOLD THE SERVANTS TO LEAVE THE GARDEN DOORS OPEN.

IT WAS A STANDARD CASE. IT WAS A STANDARD STORY:
A POOR MAN CARED FOR AN INJURED CRANE IN A SNOWSTORM, A YEAR LATER A BEAUTIFUL WOMAN GRANTED HIM PROSPERITY BEYOND HIS WILDEST DREAMS.
WHEN THE WOMAN'S TRUE NATURE WAS REVEALED, SHE WOULD TURN BACK INTO A BIRD...
I'D HEARD SOMETHING LIKE THAT BEFORE.

But leave this.

It was a gift, wasn't it?

It would be rude to take it back.

All this time...

...You thought this was my favor to you?

Oh no, you poor woman.

The sword was a gift.

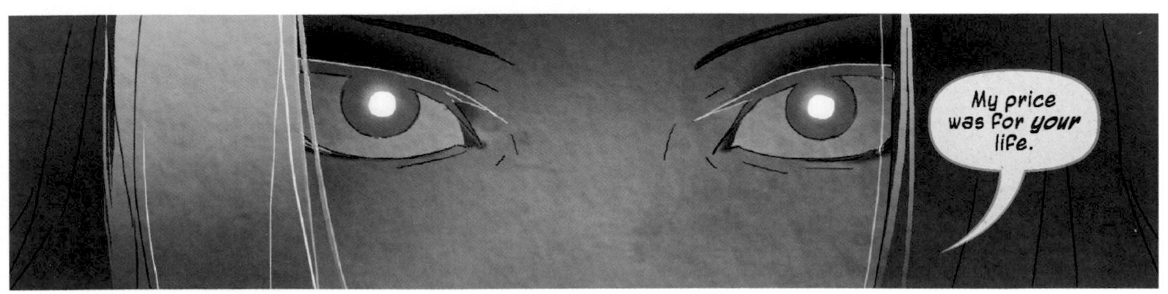
My price was for *your* life.

I GUESS MOST PEOPLE WOULD HAVE ASKED,
'WHO WOULD DO ALL THAT FOR SOME PAPER CRANES?'
I NEVER QUESTIONED IT. SPIRITS ARE ODD ABOUT THESE THINGS.
BUT SOME TIME LATER I LEARNED:
THE WIFE HAD PASSED AWAY. AND THE HOUSE HAD DECLARED A NEW MASTER...
YAMAGATA IZURU.

Oh...
Then the true master...
Once upon a time, in a deep and wild snow storm a man met an injured crane...
Once upon a time, a young girl came to a poor couple's door...
...A COMMON STORY.
...OR SO I'D THOUGHT.
...So the first of her paper cranes was a child.
Lady Mitsuru, what favor did you ask in return?
...I'D HONESTLY NEVER THOUGHT TO ASK.
END

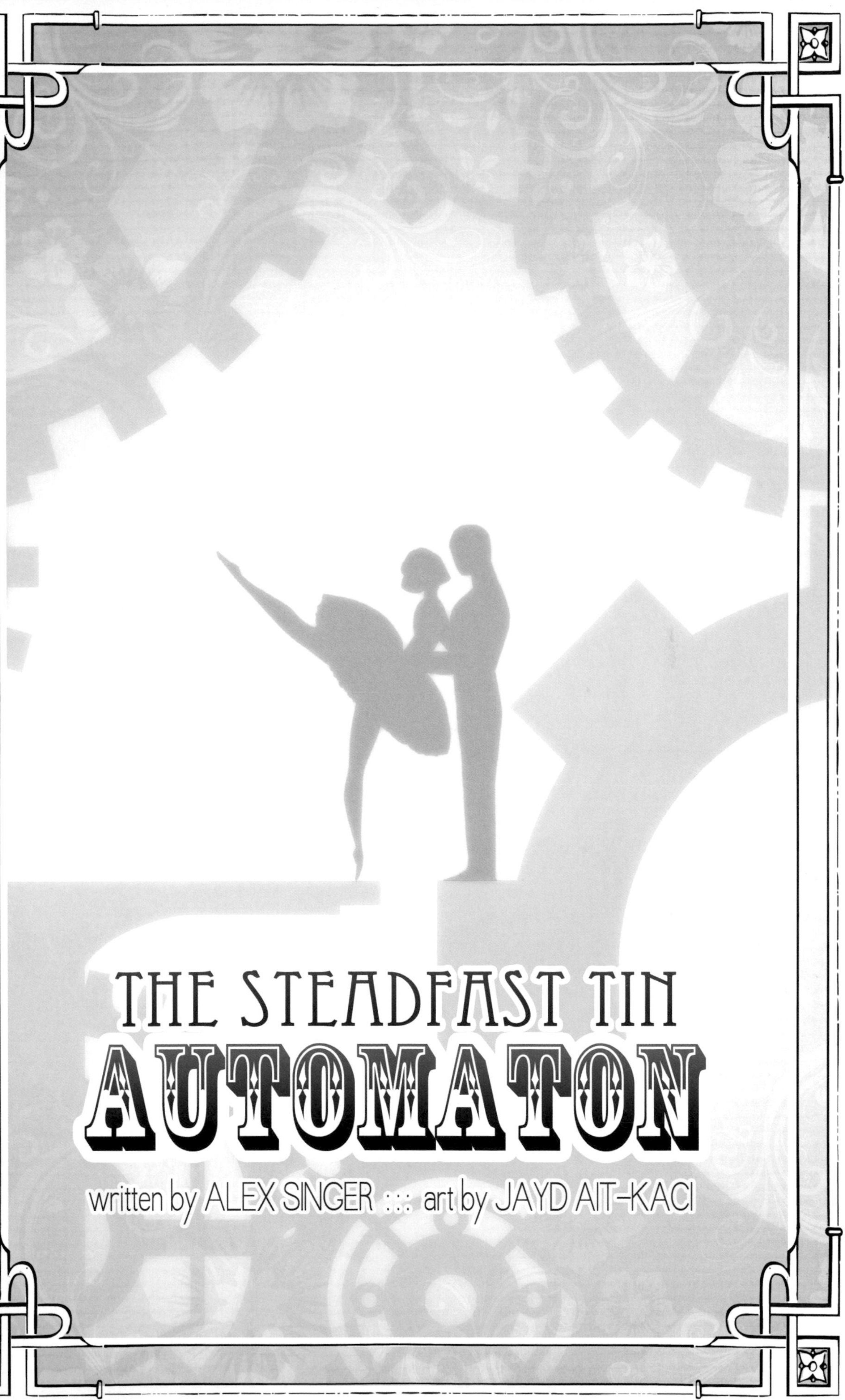
THE STEADFAST TIN
AUTOMATON
written by ALEX SINGER ::: art by JAYD AIT-KACI

They put Steinhildr in a box.

She could hardly blame them for it. It was what one did to tools that were not in use, and, besides, it was a relief from the loudness of the war.

They stored the box in a warehouse beneath an old theater. The theater stayed mostly closed for renovations, and her only visitor was an old man the owner paid to be sure no one stole any of the old costumes.

"Here now, Hilde," said the old caretaker, who was at that time the only one who called her anything but 'the unit' or 'the weapon.' "Let me just crack the lid just a bit for you. It must be terribly stuffy, and you must want to see something."

To which Steinhildr replied that she had seen quite enough, and anyway her air intakes had taken in much worse than this. Mustard gas, in particular, had been difficult to process.

The old man often left the lid cracked, anyway. His grandson had been a member of the fighting unit who had paid for her return after the war.

"Our Minerva!" they called her. "Our mighty warrior maiden." They found it a shame to scrap her, even when they brought her home and discovered they were all too broke to truly keep her.

Selling her to the theater had been a gentle compromise.

Johannes, one of the young cavalry men, had often said that the pretend wars had been much prettier. Pretty like her, he said, and her glass spun hair.

"If only this war were pretend, Hilde," he said, with a sad smile, the day before he and his horse were ripped to pieces under the fire of an enemy automaton's mounted machine gun. She had been pretty, too, that cruel French automaton, but nothing about her had been pretend.

When the renovations were close to done, the old man stopped coming. He may have died, though it was also possible that the theater had found no other use for him. Before he left, he damaged the latch on Steinhildr's box, so that it could never fully close.

"Get some air, Hilde," he told her with a wink. "You are a fine lady. You should treat yourself well."

It was the last thing he ever said to her. Steinhildr supposed he might have been fired for breaking the box, but no one ever came to fix it.

There were far more important things to concentrate on, after all. Things had suddenly gotten much busier. The other automatons rattled with excitement, for they said with its renovations finished, the theater had found a new owner.

"Someone who really wants to use us," said one of the old dancers.

"For something besides puppet shows, you think?" said another, wearing an old fashioned peasant's dress.

"Oh, more than that," sang Badin, an old gramophone. Badin had been designed to play music at spring fairs. He was little more than a mechanical head and torso, set on a stand that could be wheeled to wherever music was required. His face was molded to look like a festive clown. He knew more music than words, and so he tended to replace the lyrics of his favorite songs with dialogue. "The new owner wishes to make money, my darling. He wishes to make us a real theater, my darling, my darling."

The old man never came back, but many other people did. Many people, young and old, came to fetch things from the storehouse. Some of the stagehands were no older than Steinhildr's old unit in the war. Once or twice one of these younger stagehands would examine the box where Steinhildr was kept. When they cracked open the lid, Steinhildr would turn her glass eyes upwards.

"Good evening," she would say. "I am Steinhildr M94. What do you require of me?"

The stagehand would quickly replace the lid.

This was not to say all the automatons received such a response to their greetings: The automatons made for dancing were oiled and given new clothes. Badin was given a new paint job and a speaker which allowed his voice to carry across the whole theater should he wish it.

The automatons gossiped amongst themselves: Where had all this money come from? And from whom had all these new machines come?

"Fools, fools!" sang Badin in the beat of a children's song. "Have you not heard? One of our new patrons is the old man Hoffman. Why else do you think they've dusted us all off?"

This caused a stir among all the automatons, even Steinhildr. Hoffman was known to be one of the greatest mechanists still living, and he had been considered invaluable during the war.

No one had heard from him in a long time, and everyone wondered what he was doing pouring money into a small theater in Rosenstern.

"Not just money!" crowed Badin. "They say he has opened a new workshop. They say he wishes to return to the business!"

That seemed quite impossible, Steinhildr thought. It had been said the Master had withdrawn from building automatons after the Great War, and yet new mechanisms began to arrive, ones intended to make the stage move.

"Well, the new sets are nice, I suppose," they often said, "but who is performing?"

That question was answered on the last working day of the week. Instead of equipment and instructions, the Master sent a new automaton.

It had been quite the scene, apparently. He'd marched right into the office of the owner. He'd brought a woman wrapped in furs. She'd held his hand in a manner most observers had called fearful. No one could tell, from first glance, that she'd been a machine.

"Oh, yes," cried Badin, who had heard the fearful murmurings of the chorus automatons. "So sad, so sad. Soon we shall all be obsolete, obsolete like the spear lady who stays in her box!"

News of Hoffman's 'new doll' filtered down into the storage room, from stage hands and from irate older units. It was remarkable, they said. The Master had not lost his touch.

"Where are you going, war machine?" the other theater-owned automatons had once asked her when, once a week at midnight, Steinhildr would slide the lid off her box and push her way out.

They held rehearsals that evening, even though all of the workers had gone home. Steinhildr heard the 'tap, tap, tap' on the ceiling above, as she had heard it for the past three nights since the new automaton arrived.

It was this tapping that Steinhildr followed up the steps from the storeroom. She maneuvered carefully – her right leg had suffered damage from a machine gun, and moved just a half a second more slowly than the left. She followed the sound and the light from the small lantern lit on the stage. Sheets had been thrown over most of the new onstage mechanisms, except Badin, who played an old wordless instrumental.

In the space where the crew passed between performances, she first saw her.

The new automaton did not wear white. Her skin, or the surface that had been crafted to look like skin, was pale enough to suffice. She wore a dress of plain grey, one that lay tight around her waist and flowed around her legs. It showed how she moved.

Oh, how she moved! The automaton stood only on one leg, with the second extended behind her. She wore no stocking, so as to show off the silver and black joints under each knee. She tipped in a motion not unlike a water pump. When the toe of her raised leg, sharp and tipped in silver, swept down across floor, swinging the new automaton across the room in a swell of Badin's song, Steinhildr regretted the comparison. The automaton's waist twisted with as much grace as any war machine.

Her sharp toes plucked the floor boards. Her arms stretched at either side of her like a bird. Steinhildr leaned forward to catch her better in her sights.

This was her mistake. Her bad knee bumped a beam propped against the wall. She caught it before it fell, but the end scraped the floorboards, and that was enough.

The new automaton's heels sank back to the floor. Her body swiveled in one clean motion. Steinhildr saw her face. It was round, well-carved, and full of a shock.

"Who's there?" called the dancer, in a sweet voice. It carried only the slightest of mechanical accents.

Steinhildr gave no answer. She retreated, with the utmost haste, back to her storage room and her box. She spent the rest of that night there in silence, as she had so many years before.

"War machine, war machine, where have you been?" Badin had no illusions of who had been snooping about backstage that night.

Steinhildr ignored his song. "What model was she? I did not see a number on her."

Badin found these questions ridiculous, and hummed as much. "Hah! No model number. She is one of a kind, our fine Coppelia," he sang. "One of a kind, not like you and all your sisters, Miss 94."

Steinhildr was not interested in her own designations. "How does she move?"

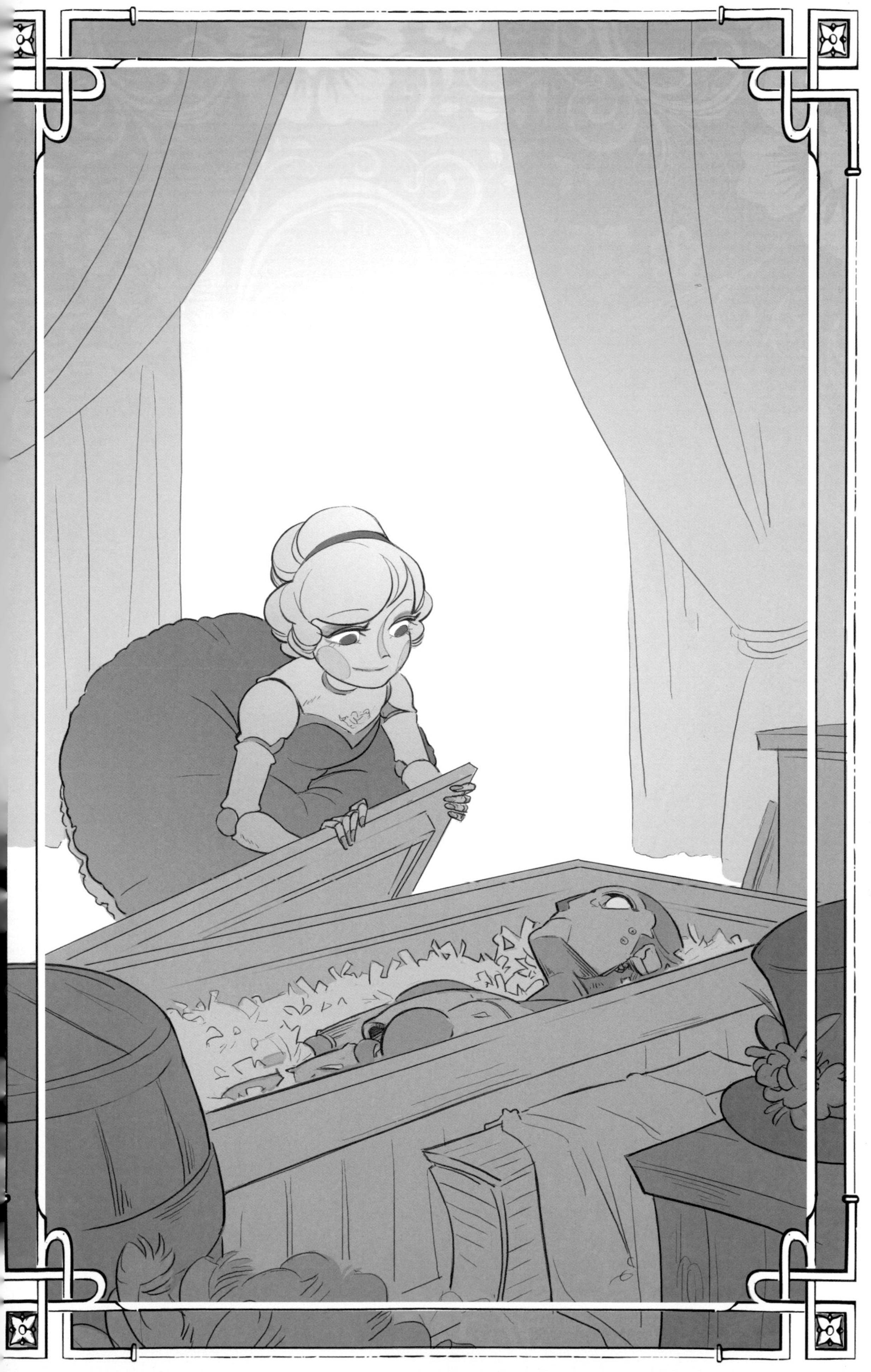

"Much more fleetly than you, honorable war machine," answered Badin. "But how odd of you to ask such things! Who knew, two-three, that you, two-three, could think of things besides your past glories?"

He set that last question to an old victory march.

Steinhildr let out a deep breath from her chambers. "No," she said, because Badin was incorrect. There were no glories to consider. "What do you think she is?"

"She is Coppelia," sang Badin, in children's nursery rhyme.

Coppelia. Coppelia. He said other things, after that, but the name was all Steinhildr heard.

The performance was a rousing success. Steinhildr did not see it, but others spoke of it quite a bit.

"They were beside themselves with shock and awe," said the chorus automaton, sourly. "Of course they were. It was new and incomprehensible. People love things that are new and incomprehensible. The theater is saved. This is the worst."

"The worst?" sang Badin. "But I should think you would be happy."

"It means I will have to keep being her set piece," huffed the automaton. "I should nearly rather climb into the box that frightful war machine sleeps in."

"They are mocking me," thought Steinhildr, but she found she could not think much of it. The performance had been a success. That meant there would be another.

They moved Steinhildr's box backstage. They gave her new water, oiled her joints, and measured her for a new costume. They combed her hair. They gave her a fake spear. It was amongst this fuss that Steinhildr heard from the other automatons again, as they milled about waiting for their own assignments.

"All this fuss for that piece of tubing," muttered a member of the chorus. "What good is it being 'almost human?' No offense, Leopold."

"Quite all right," said one of the dressers, who was quite friendly with the automatons. "I quite agree, you know. It leaves us uneasy too, you know, seeing her shift about like that. That is Hoffman's thing, I suppose."

"I suppose Hoffman must somehow occupy himself, since there will be no more wars for him. Still, I wish he could entertain himself elsewhere. Why here? Do you know?"

"They say that Rosenstern was a boyhood home of his," said Leopold, "but I've heard that some important people are visiting the old estate in the north."

The chorus loved a bit of fleshy intrigue.

"Important people? Do you mean political people? " one asked.

"Does Hoffman think he will impress them again?" asked another. "Everyone remembers those horrors he created during the war! Oh, ah, no offense to any possible present company!"

They had forgotten about Steinhildr and her box.

"Present company forgives you," said a new voice, one clear, wry, and almost human. "But present company should think you are being awful rude."

Steinhildr nearly shifted with surprise. She recognized the feet that walked into the room then. She could hear the members of the chorus stumble, and Leopold dropped his measuring stick.

"Coppelia!" said Leopold. "Your fitting was scheduled for this afternoon—"

"I know," said Coppelia, quite ignoring the fumbling of the automatons around her. "I'm sorry to be a bother about this, but Father wants to be sure the weight of my costume will not offset my routine."

"Ah, that will be tricky," stumbled Leopold. "It hasn't been brought up yet—"

"Could it be brought up now?" asked Coppelia. "I would hate to disappoint Father. He is very set in these things."

The threat of Hoffman's displeasure was enough to cause Leopold to rush off to the basement. The automatons shuffled off to the stage. It left Coppelia alone.

She knelt beside Steinhildr's box.

"You might have said something," said Coppelia. "It is cruel of them to speak of you with so little respect. You have seen far more than them."

Steinhildr said nothing. She saw fingers curl in the crack of the lid.

"I wish you would speak to me, at least," said Coppelia. "I have decided I'd like to be the sort of performer who speaks to my fans. You watch my rehearsals, don't you? You are very loyal, if you're willing to sit through all that."

Still, Steinhildr said nothing.

"You move to the beat of a march," noted Coppelia. "I could hear it in your steps. That is how I knew it must be someone who once went to war. Badin says this next performance will be all about war. At least tell me your name?"

'Steinhildr M94' is what the answer ought to have been, but Steinhildr could make out the faint sliver of Coppelia's wide, worried eyes.

"Hilde," she said.

"Hilde," said Coppelia. She sounded it out with such life in her words that the war machine knew she could never be called 'Steinhildr' again. "Ah, what a gentle name. How lovely, Hilde. I am Coppelia. It is a great pleasure to meet you, my first fan. Please, do come again tonight if you are able. I should like to see you, and not your box."

"But, oh, my dear, you have a gentleman caller!" sang Badin, with clear dislike.

“Hush Badin,” said Coppelia. “I invited her.”

“A spy!” sang Badin. “A phantom, lurking in the wings...”

“Badin, you must be tired,” said Coppelia, and pulled the cloth over his head.

Hilde waited until his gears had wound into their sleeping positions before she spoke. “What he has said is perfectly correct.”

Coppelia pivoted towards the sound of her voice.

“Please, do forgive him,” said Coppelia. “I know most think he is a bother, but he makes music for me.”

“He thinks you are beautiful,” said Hilde, quietly. “He shall sing you whatever song you would like.”

Coppelia smiled and shook her head.

“I’m not so sure of that,” said Coppelia. Her eyes dimmed, faintly. “When Father is here, he sings what he likes. Oh, please come into the light. I’d love to see you.”

“You cannot see me as I am?” asked Hilde, in some confusion.

“I was not built to see in the dark!” laughed Coppelia, brightening. “But, you obviously were. How lucky you are.”

Carefully, Hilde pushed forward into the circle of light afforded by Coppelia’s lamp. She moved slowly, mindful of the drag on her damaged leg.

Coppelia’s eyes lit a touch brighter. “Oh, look at you!” She ran to her, her hands fluttering in the air just above Hilde’s elbows. “I have never seen one of my father’s war models. Not that I think you are old— But, oh! Your arms—”

Hilde felt the senses in her eyes turn in rapid focus at the sudden flurry around her. “I am older,” she said.

“No, but I am being rude,” said Coppelia, knotting her hands in front of her. Her hands were much better articulated, filled with a dozen little, silver joints.

“You have my permission,” said Hilde.

Coppelia tilted gratefully. She ran her hands up Hilde’s arms with all the care and curiosity of an engineer. “Is it true that you have interchangeable parts?

“Yes,” said Hilde.

“And you can lift twice your weight?”

“Four times my weight,” said Hilde. “Yes.”

“You would be able to lift me, then. I am not reinforced like you,” said Coppelia. “Can this armor come off?”

“Yes,” said Hilde.

Coppelia paused. "...That was a very unfortunate question, wasn't it."

"No," said Hilde.

"You are teasing me." There was a faint hint of a laugh in Coppelia's vocalizer. "Dance with me."

All of Hilde's process wound to a momentary halt as she processed that request. "Dance?"

"Yes," said Coppelia.

"I cannot," said Hilde.

"You can march, can't you?"

"That is very different."

"Not so much," said Coppelia. "I should like to know how to dance with a soldier, and you, you are more a soldier than any other I have ever met."

"You should not wish for such things," said Hilde.

"I will show you," said Coppelia. She held out a hand.

Coppelia pulled the cloth off of Badin. She asked him to play a song.

"That siege engine is meant for things more lethal than this," he hummed.

"Don't be so silly, Badin," said Coppelia.

So she danced with Hilde. She guided one hand to her jointed waist and extended the other outwards. Her fingers held the perfect pressure. They shifted along Hilde's arm, her still hand, with a subtlety and nervous energy she would not expected of an automaton. Yet when she pulled near, Hilde could hear her central pumps. They worked with a steady beat that was not all that much different than a human heart. Not at all.

"Please come again," said Coppelia. "Father will be seeing me tomorrow, but the night after, I want to see you."

"I should not distract you," said Hilde.

"It is not a distraction," said Coppelia. "You don't have to answer just now, but do come."

Hilde went back to her box, but she found she could not lie so still.

"Do come," Coppelia had said. Do come. Please come again.

She played the sound in her head, again, and again.

They said the performance was sold out. Hilde supposed it must have been. She had detected at least three hundred and forty-six individual heartbeats in filing into the seats, which meant that the theater had been filled to capacity.

"And where is our star?" muttered the chorus automatons, with great distaste. They all waited in the wings. "In her dressing room? Who does she think she is, an actress? Leopold, are you sure this is on right?"

"I have refastened it three times," said Leopold. He had finished with Hilde's play armor a few minutes ago. "You should be glad. They say the men from the north estate have come tonight. They say they're in the front row, and Hoffman—"

From his spot behind the stage, Badin's humming ceased.

"Good evening," said Hilde. "Master Hoffman."

"Good evening," said the man, who had been waiting in the door.

"Good evening," said Leopald, in some alarm. "I am sorry, Master Hoffman, you must wish to see the director—"

"I have no interest in you," said Hoffman, in a high voice that scratched like a record. He wore a narrow grey suit and clutched a wicked black cane.

Leopald backed out the door. Hoffman snapped his cane against the wooden floor and paced along the row of waiting automatons, who stood as straight and as proper as they could under his attentions.

He stopped in front of Hilde.

"M94," he said. "Steinhildr. Correct?"

"That is what I was called," said Hilde.

"Odd response," said Hoffman, pacing around her. He plucked at her costume and frowned. "What have they put you in – nevermind that. You are not in bad condition. Your higher processes are obviously working. Heavens, but you are old. And so heavy! What was I thinking, giving you all of that armor?"

Hilde's response was carefully automated. "My armor is designed to repel heavy artillery fire—"

Hoffman held up a hand. "I was not looking for an answer," he said. "I have not seen an M94 unit in some years. It is funny that I should find you here. Do you know why it is so funny?"

"Shall I answer that, Master Hoffman?" asked Hilde. Automatons began to file out. Badin began to sing. Hoffman raised his eyebrows.

"I will tell you," he said, with a sigh. "I got my start building your type for puppet shows. That sort that played the streets when I was a boy. Your prototype hit fake dragons over the head and the children laughed at her. She was so good at striking fake dragons that I built her up to fight real ones. Then they put their dragons to bed and threw her away. There should have been no place for you in this world, but here you are, doing puppet shows again. It must be very boring for you."

"It is adequate, Master Hoffman."

The Master's eyes turned hard. "Don't simper. She mentioned you."

There was an edge in his voice. Hilde felt her targeting scopes activate.

He noticed, of course. He put his hand on her arm and laughed. "No, no, don't bother getting alarmed," he said. "I do not mind. In fact, I mind your meddling so little I will buy you off of this silly place when our run is over. Aren't you fortunate? You should thank me, Steinhildr. You are about to have purpose again."

The response came whether Hilde had meant it or not. "Thank you, Master Hoffman."

The stage began to creak and move. The lights changed, casting the top of Hoffman's face in shadow as his lips pulled into a line. It was not quite a smile. He patted Hilde on her arm and left.

The music played. The curtains rose. Steinhildr marched. Coppelia danced.

In the front row sat a row of the important men from the northern estates. They had shiny boots and long coats. They watched the proceedings with great interest, murmuring amongst themselves.

Between acts the audience roared with applause, but Steinhildr had been made to hear many things through the din of war. She could hear what the men said, as their eyes gleamed and their boots creaked on the old, wooden floors.

"That dancing one is perfect," said the first.

"She is of great interest to us," said the second. "Of course, with some modifications..."

"Tell me what customizations you would like me to make," said Hoffman, in the flicking shadow of his automaton's dance.

That night, as the cast and crew celebrated, Badin sang a new song. "How fortunate! How fortunate we are!" he crowed, between verses. "For all that we have lost will be found again soon! How fortunate for Coppelia, how fortunate for our country!"

He sang to the beat of a march. He was still attached to the sound machine. His voice echoed from every corner of the theater, as loud as any drum.

When Hilde found Coppelia that evening, there was no music playing at all. She sat in the center of the stage, with her legs folded close to her chassis. The old oil lamp flickered faintly. Hilde hung back, just out of the light.

"Please, come," said Coppelia, her vocalizers at their lowest setting.

"Do you wish to dance?" asked Hilde, sliding forward.

Coppelia tilted her head, as though considering. Then, she slid her hand into Hilde's, she levered herself off the floor.

"Before I came here," said Coppelia, as they moved. "I lived with my father in a university. I do not remember so much from that time, but I do remember that there was a student. A young man. He worked for my father, sometimes, and I think he thought that I was human."

"Did it bother you?" asked Hilde.

"I didn't know what being bothered was!" Coppelia laughed, in spite of herself. Her shoulders moved with it. Hilde wondered how she had learned to do that. "But he bothered my father. 'You do not have time for such things,' Father would say to me. Then one day the student... stopped."

"He stopped coming?"

"He stopped," said Coppelia. "Tell me about the Great War."

Soft music began to play. The opening chords of a waltz. Hilde blinked, unused to the sudden change in topic. "There is not much worth saying."

"Can you lie?" asked Coppelia, with interest.

"No," admitted Hilde. "There is really not much to say. I knew a student, too. I knew many students. They were very young. They called me their Minerva. Their battle maiden. Most of them died."

"How did they die?" asked Coppelia.

"The trenches were wet," said Hilde. "I was proofed against moisture. They were not. Their vent systems would get clogged from wetness, and sometimes also gas. They would lie down in the mud and stop moving. Some died in the advance. They would catch on barbed wire. It would hold them and tear them, while the enemy automatons shot at them. If my guns jammed, they would be torn to pieces before I could return fire."

"That can't be right," said Coppelia. "No one dies like that on a battlefield."

"Not in the battles you have known," said Hilde. Her eyes refocused.

Coppelia went quiet. Her feet slowed. Her hand tightened on Hilde's shoulder.

"Those men," she said, finally. "They want to make me into a war automaton. They said that I will be a beautiful valkyrie, and that my country will love me. Do you think I would be as good at war?"

Hilde stepped away from Coppelia. She observed her smooth joints, and the careful tilt of her head.

"You would be as good at war as you are at dancing," said Hilde.

"Ah," said Coppelia, pivoting with expert care. She led Hilde through four more steps. "Hilde. You are not so bad at dancing."

"That is kind of you to say."

"Did no one ever tell you that?" asked Coppelia.

"Never, before I met you."

"Hilde," said Coppelia. "I do not want to go to war."

Hilde stopped. Coppelia bumped into her. Her metal knee clicked against Hilde's softly. Hilde steadied her, both hands resting on the other automaton's narrow, pale shoulders She pushed a strand of Coppelia's glass-spun hair away from her face. "You would be surprised," said Hilde, "how seldom men will check inside a box."

The music grew louder. Hilde froze. She had not noticed it until just then. As they stood still, the waltz grew faster, the crackling music combined into a voice, and through the theater a shrill voice began to shout, in time: "No! No! No!"

"Badin," said Coppelia.

"My sweet Coppelia!" cried the gramophone. His voice echoed from all corners. Hilde turned her head rapidly to find him, but it was no use. His voice came from every corner of the stage. "You would not leave me, would you?"

"Badin!" said Coppelia. "Please, be quiet!"

"My sweet Coppelia!" cried Badin, as the fixtures began to rock. The old oil lamp jittered. Up above pieces of the set tore loose. "Don't you want to be a hero?"

"Badin, be silent!" said Coppelia.

"You would let yourself be stolen?"

"Badin!"

"Thief!" cried Badin. The sound grew louder. The stage shook and groaned. Hilde saw him, sitting amongst the wooden trees. His face looked bigger than it had before, and though his smile stayed the same as it always had, his eyes glared down at them in hate. His voice had lost all music in it: it was nothing but the shrill, sharp shout like men on the radio. "Idiots! Fools! Traitors!"

Hilde threw the oil lamp at those burning eyes.

They say that the theater was too stubborn to burn, although it took several hours to bring the fires under control. They say that, it in the end, the damage was not so severe.

Less fortunate were the owners of the theater, who had lost their new stage equipment in the blaze. They blamed a forgotten lamp and poor security. That their new patrons refused to pay to replace the items burned. They closed the theater for repairs. It was closed for a very long time.

'And what a pity that was!' said the townsfolk. There had been much talk of the theater's new show the night it had burned down. Of course, the average townsfolk soon forgot about the stories and the rumors related to the theater and its new mechanical star.

They forgot about the men who had visited the north estate, as well. They had more pressing day to day concerns, but every now and again it would come up as a choice piece of gossip: Do you remember what they planned to do with that old theater? Do you remember that toy dancer, Coppelia?

It was said of course that Coppelia was lost in the fire. Hoffman moved on nearly as quickly as he had come.

What a pity, the people would say as they passed the closed theater. They should just get that pair from New York. Oh, haven't you heard? A pair of automatons who do their own dancing. It is said they are the 'big thing' in America. They just did a show in New York. Oh, no, I don't know the name of it. It's a pity they waste themselves someplace like that. Imagine if they were to come here, where they might be appreciated.

Imagine what a show it might be. Imagine the things that they could do.

the flower in the Gravel
BY ANGELICA MARIA LOPEZ

IN A FAR AWAY LAND,
THERE WAS A TALE OF A DREADFUL DRAGON THAT ROAMED THE LAND.
A DRAGON RUMORED TO HAVE GREAT TREASURE HIDDEN AWAY FROM ALL.

IN AN OLD ABANDONED TOWER ON THE EDGE OF THE GRASSLANDS.

MANY HAVE TRIED TO CONQUER THE TOWER.

BUT ALL HAVE RETURNED EMPTY-HANDED.

'NO TREASURE IS WORTH BRAVING THE DRAGON'S TRAPS!' QUOTED A FAIR KNIGHT FROM THE TOWN OF DAWNSPEAK.
IT SEEMS LIKE THE DRAGON'S WIT OUTMATCHED OUR OWN, AND THUS THE TOWER HAS FALLEN OUT OF POPULARITY WITH ADVENTURERS WHO SEEK QUICK FAME AND FORTUNE.

WHO WRITES LIKE THIS?

I GUESS IT DOESN'T MATTER ANYMORE, I'M HERE ALREADY.
IF I HAVE NO COMPETITION, THEN THIS SHOULD BE A PIECE OF CAKE!

SHINK!!!
I JUST
HAVE TO
MAKE MY WAY
THROUGH ALL OF THESE TRAPS?!
Cough
Cough
SERIOUSLY?! WHO PUT THESE HERE?!

AH!

FINALLY!!
THE DRAGON'S TREASURE WILL SOON BE MINE!

OH.
I'M-
I'M SORRY! AM I IN THE WRONG DUNGEON?
AGAIN?

HOLD ON.
LET ME TAKE A LOOK.
DID I SCREW UP...?

U-UM ...

NO, YOU'RE IN THE RIGHT PLACE.

BUT... I'M SORRY. THERE'S NO DRAGON'S TREASURE HERE!
What?!

LOOK, I'M NOT HERE TO ARGUE BUT HAVE YOU SEEN THOSE TRAPS?!
I NEARLY DIED GETTING HERE!

JUST HOW DID YOU GET PAST THOSE?
I'UNNO. DUMB LUCK?

I MAINTAIN THOSE TRAPS. ISN'T IT OBVIOUS? THEY'RE A WORK OF ART!

EACH ONE IS DELICATELY PUT TOGETHER AND CLEANED. DUNGEONS CAN GET QUITE DIRTY WITHOUT LOVE.

BUT THAT CAN BE SAID FOR ANY DWELLING. SEE, THOUGH? THERE'S NO TREA-

WAIT, HOLD ON.
IF THERE'S NO TREASURE,
WHY DO YOU LIVE HERE?

IT COULDN'T HAVE LASTED FOREVER...

YOU'D THINK A DRAGON WOULD HAVE MADE THEIR APPEARANCE BY NOW, IS THAT IT?

THERE MOST DEFINITELY WAS ONE HERE. FOR A LONG TIME SHE GRACED THESE SKIES.

BUT.

THAT STOPPED...

WHEN SHE FOUND ME.

WHEN I...

WAS RESCUED.

I THOUGHT THAT WAS THE END OF MY FAIRY TALE.

BUT LET ME SHOW YOU INSTEAD-

I'M SORRY I TOOK SO LONG.

WE HAD GUESTS TODAY.

SEE, THOUGH?

THERE'S NO TREASURE HERE.

NOT ANYMORE.

OH.

IT HAPPENED LAST WEEK. DRAGONS DON'T LIVE VERY LONG THESE DAYS.
NOT WITH HOW THE WORLD KEEPS *CHANGING.*
I'M SORRY...
SO YOU STAYED HERE BY YOURSELF? SINCE THEN?

YES.
I COULDN'T JUST LEAVE HER.
THE HUMAN WORLD HAS NOTHING FOR ME.

THAT'S SO SAD...
BUT- I WONDER WHY THE RUMORS STARTED UP AGAIN THOUGH ...?

Y-YOU KNOW-
WHAT IF-
M-MAYBE THE DRAGON WAS PROTECTING A TREASURE AFTER ALL?

IT DOESN'T HAVE TO ALWAYS BE GOLD AND SILVER.
YOU KNOW, MAYBE THE DRAGON'S TREASURE WAS SOMETHING **MORE?**
SO I THINK- MAYBE...

...YOU SHOULD LIVE THE LIFE YOU WERE GIVEN.
HUH?
IT WAS VALUABLE TO THE DRAGON, RIGHT?

I MEAN, LOOK AT ALL OF THIS! THERE'S SO MUCH OUT THERE!

IT'S OKAY IF YOU NEED TIME TO MOURN,
BUT THERE'S MORE FOR YOU OUT THERE, TOO.
SO MUCH TO LEARN AND EXPERIENCE, Y'KNOW?

THAT'S WHAT I THINK, ANYWAY.

YOU DON'T HAVE TO DO IT ALONE, IF YOU DON'T WANT TO.

... YOU'RE SO STRANGE.
TO THINK YOU BESTED MY TRAPS JUST TO END UP HERE LIKE THIS...

NAH, THAT'S COO-
WHOA!!

I'M SO GLAD. I CAN FINALLY REST.
YOU'VE GROWN SO MUCH, TULIP.

BABA ...
I WAS WORRIED ABOUT LEAVING YOU ALL ALONE...

I'M SORRY. THIS IS ALL I CAN DO FOR YOU.
THANK YOU FOR ANSWERING MY PLEA-
TO SAVE MY TREASURE, ADVENTURER

WHOA!

HOLY MOLY!
CHECK OUT THOSE SWEET DOUBLOONS!

HEY NOW!
IT'S ALL YOURS!
WHAT DO YOU PLAN TO DO WITH IT?

I-
I DON'T KNOW.
TAKE YOUR TIME.

A FEW MONTHS LATER...

OH MY GOSH!
THIS NEW DUNGEON-TRAINING PROGRAM LOOKS REALLY COOL!
I HEAR SOME OF THE TRAPS ARE TO DIE FOR!

I'M REALLY EXCITED FOR THIS!
WHO KNEW THIS LITTLE TOWN COULD BECOME SO HIP!?

BUSINESS WAS BOOMING IN THIS LITTLE TOWN.
AND I FOUND WORK SOON ENOUGH

EVERYONE WAS ABUZZ ABOUT THE NEW, MODERN DUNGEON-TRAINING TOWER.
ADVENTURER'S CAME FROM FAR AND WIDE TO EXPERIENCE IT.
SONYA! THERE YOU ARE!
CAN YOU SUMMON THE BOSS FOR ME?
SURE! LEAVE IT TO ME!

TULIP!

THE CROWD'S WAITING FOR YOU DOWNSTAIRS.

YOU SHOULD GO SEE THEM BEFORE THEY GET ROWDY.

IF YOU'RE FEELING UP TO IT, I MEAN!
OH.
NO-

YOU'RE RIGHT, I SHOULD GO DO THAT.
I'M SURPRISED... EVERYONE LIKES MY TRAPS.
CAN YOU-
LEAD THE WAY, SONYA?
YEAH! OF COURSE!
LET'S GO!

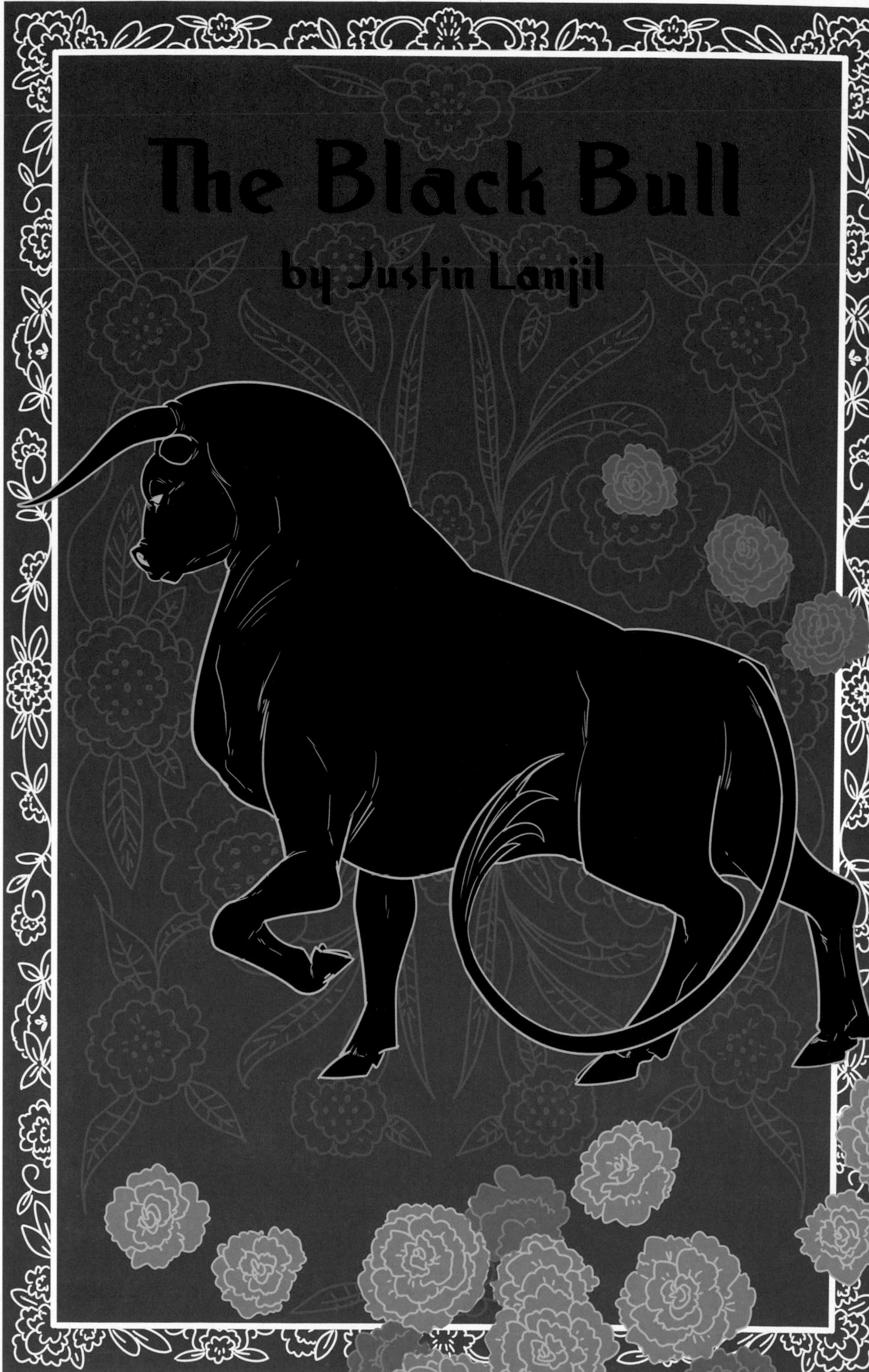
The Black Bull
by Justin Lanjil

Cough

My thanks for your hospitality and shelter.
I have no money to repay your kindess.
Allow me to leave you with words to guide your future.

Each morning, look out the window behind the house.
You three will all find the road to your fortune waiting.

I offer you my aid.

I swear that no harm shall come to you while I am by your side.

If you wish, climb on my back.

A demon lurks in this valley.
Watch the sky and wait.
If the blue brightens, then the demon is slain and it is safe.
But if the sky turns red, I have lost and you must not venture near.

It's you!

You've had a long journey.
Come in.

Rest here as long as you need
My daugher will help dress your wounds.

Where is the bull?

That's-
I-I'm...

When I was young, a curse was placed on me.
My mother's magic could protect me in this home-
-but outside, I was transformed into that beastly form.
I believe my mother sent me to you in hopes of breaking the curse.

Then-

You're here and safe.
With me.

LADY TILDA AND THE DRAGON

BY: SARA GOETTER

Dear Lady Tilda,
Out far into the mountains is a great and terrible dragon that's terrorizing nearby villages. I have sent many knights before you, but none have returned. You are our last hope!
Slay the dragon!
-The King

CRUNCH

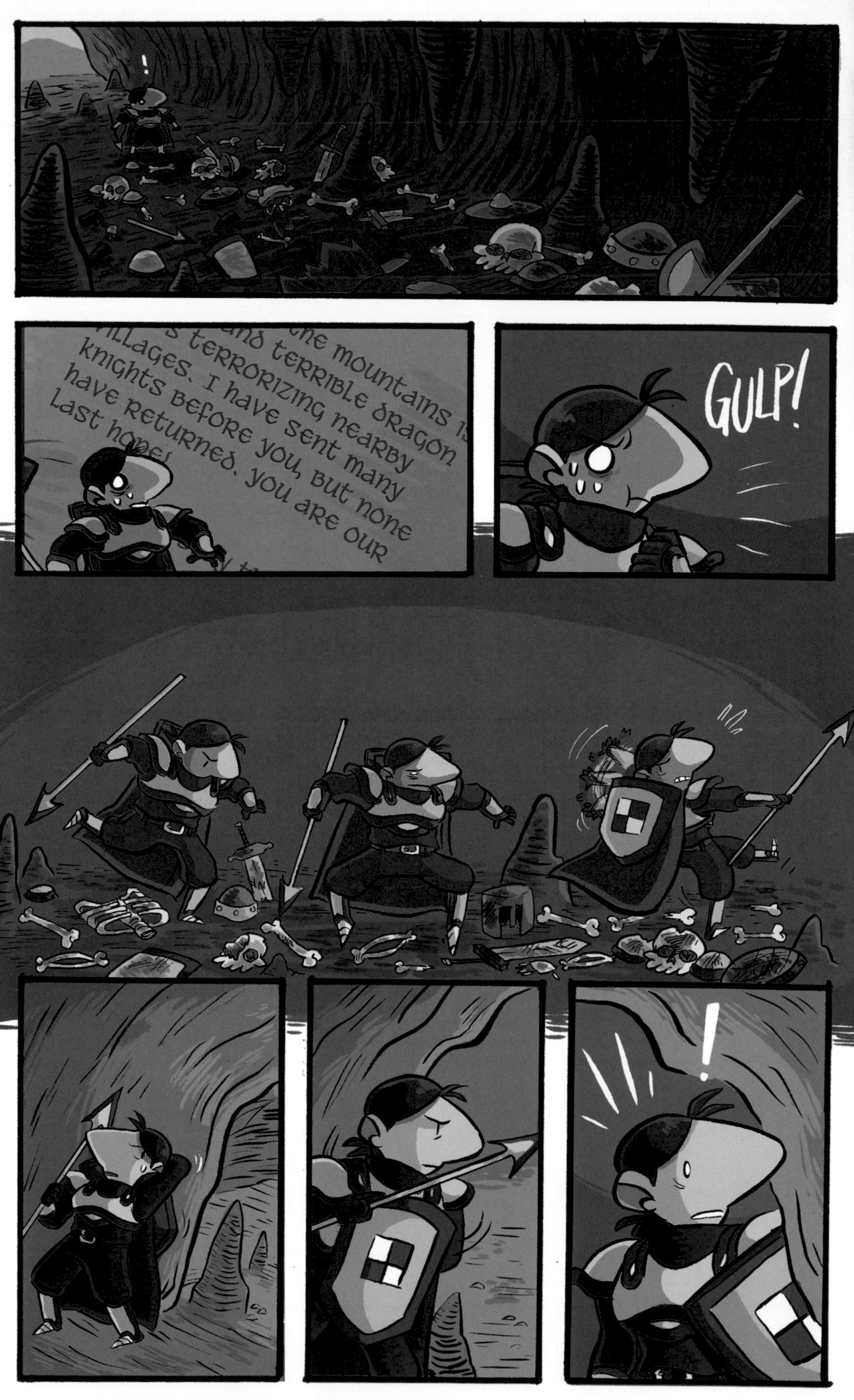
!
the mountains
and terrible dragon
terrorizing nearby
villages. I have sent many
knights before you, but none
have returned. You are our
last hope!
GULP!
!

SNIFF

×!!
FWOOM

HUFF
HUFF
!

CLANG!

?

hic
sniff
?

✕

WAHHHHHHHHH
SHHHHHHHHHHHH
WAHHHHHHHHA
SHHHHHHHHHH

SNIFF
?
X

!

?

SNIFF

NOD
NOD

THE END

Eggchild

Story by Ash Barnes | Art by Elena "Yamino" Barbarich

In the midst of the hot season and a terrible drought, in a land where all the seasons were hot and all the droughts similarly terrible, a girl named Zahra looked up at her mother and said, "Mama, I'm hungry."

"Hungry is a reasonable thing to be, my little love," said Zahra's mother wearily, looking out the door of their hut. She and Zahra lived in a great grass sea, and the fields Zahra's mother had tended for months and months were brown and barren, the crop wilted down to bundles of sticks and rattling leaves. Heat glittered like a gauzy fluttering web on the horizon. Zahra and her mother had to content themselves with digging up hard, knobby roots from beneath the earth to eat. They tasted quite awful, but now even the roots were in short supply. Zahra's belly ached for missing them.

Zahra's mother rubbed her daughter's head, brushing her thumb behind her ear where Zahra liked it best. Then she kissed Zahra on both cheeks and said, getting up, "I will go out and look for something to eat, yes I will, yes I will. So long as I live no child of mine will sit about starving, this I promise."

Zahra only knew that starving was what had happened to her father some scattered seasons ago. He was buried under the earth like all the hard, knobby roots. She remembered him as but an echo of booming laughter, thunder in the sky, a hard shivery pressure up behind her heart.

Zahra rolled to her feet. She tugged her mother's hand. "I'll go with you!" she said.

"No, no," said Zahra's mother, and kissed her again. "No, my little love. Stay here. One of us must have the strength to cook what I bring back, yes?"

And oh, but Zahra was tired when she thought about it, heavy in her elbows and trembly in her knees. "Yes, Mama," she said.

She fetched the carrying sling and helped her mother strap it across her chest, and from the door of their hut Zahra watched her mother walk out into the swaying yellow grasses. She watched a long, long time, until her eyes watered the hollows of her cheeks, until the shimmery smudge of her mother's silhouette blurred to match all the others in the yawning distance.

Zahra took herself to bed. The light changed color in the window of the hut, first orange, then shy creeping russet.

"Like a good mango," Zahra said into the quiet, "red, red, all red," and she fell asleep dreaming of fruit, bushels and bushels of blushing ripe mangoes, her tongue moving against her teeth, her mouth open and hopeful.

Hours later, a hand found her shoulder and shook it. Zahra started awake and looked up: the hut's window was full of twinkling pinprick stars. In the darkness a shadow moved. The shadow whispered, "My little love, look, look. You won't starve, didn't I promise?"

"Mama?" said Zahra, fumbling for flint and striker. Her mother—because that's who the shadow was—found them first, and she dragged them together and made sparks leap onto the kindling in the hut's firepit. Soon little flames had joined their hot yellow hands together. They went dancing about in the dried leaves. Light eeled across the walls of the hut in ribbons, and Zahra's mother beamed down at her daughter, trembling and sweating, her smile a wide white moon's slice floating in the fragile dark.

"Look," Zahra's mother said again. "Look what I found, Zahra. We're saved, we're saved."

Her carrying sling hung huge and bulging and taut over her lap. She opened it. She showed

Zahra what was inside.

"An egg!" said Zahra, but saying that felt like saying *cat* when looking at a leopard.

The egg was enormous, bigger than both of Zahra's hands with all the fingers spread out: bigger than her head and her chest, bigger than the swooping breadth of her shoulders. It was blue the same way the dawn sky is blue, flecked with chips of shimmering violet and swirled pale, pale pink toward its tapering top. Zahra touched it with tentative fingertips and could only yank her hand back, yelping her shock.

"Mama!" she cried. "It's so hot!" And the egg was hot, hot as the hut's dooryard come early afternoon; hot as dry, dry ground wormed through with cracks; hot as bits of quartz left to glow and gleam in a window.

Though she was so desperately hungry that her stomach rolled up rumbling under her ribs, Zahra looked fretfully at the egg. She stared at it, at its colors, its semblance to the sky: she hovered her hand over it again, marveling at its insistent radiant heat. A thread of unease spun its spool over her heart.

"Mama, where did you find it?" she asked. And she added, "Maybe... maybe we shouldn't eat it. It seems special." What she meant was that it seemed so special that someone—or something—might miss it, and come looking for it.

Zahra's mother's mouth tightened into a thin line. "It's special enough to feed you, yes. A blessing is what it is," she said, "a gift," and out came the cooking skillet, settled on a grate over the hut's little fire. Hefting the egg in her hands, Zahra's mother said a final time, "A gift. Life."

She cracked it open. The yolk spilled out liquid and runny and golden, the same as any ordinary egg. It cooked like an ordinary egg and smelled like an ordinary egg, and it tasted like an ordinary egg but better, if only because Zahra had not had ordinary eggs in such a long, long time. She and her mother sat huddled around the fire in their hut and they ate the egg, every bite. They licked the shell afterward, even.

When it was gone, Zahra and her mother crawled into their blankets and folded themselves into each other's arms, watching the fire die. The shards of the egg lay scattered around the embers. Zahra picked up the largest shard, like a broken bit of the sky, and cradled it in her palms, and felt the last bit of warmth in the shell fade away to nothing.

Her stomach full but her heart in a strange agony, Zahra closed her eyes.

Her mother said then into the darkness, "There was another egg. I could not carry both."

Zahra's stomach pitched and rolled. She was afraid without being able to explain why. "Leave it," she whispered to her mother. "Leave it alone. One was enough. We'll find other food, Mama. Please? Please leave it alone?"

Zahra's mother kissed her ear. She squeezed Zahra under the blankets and sighed... and said nothing.

Two days later, a monster flew down and snatched Zahra's mother into the sky as she tried to steal the second egg. Small blessings: Zahra didn't see it happen. She was digging in the earth near the hut looking for still more roots, and her mother had gone away to forage again despite Zahra's pleas. A trio of travelers crossing the great grass sea had glimpsed the whole thing, however, and when they came upon Zahra's hut and Zahra herself later, they described it to her well enough.

"The monster's wings blocked out the sun," said one.

"It made a terrible screeching, screaming noise," said the other, "and the noise was almost like words."

"This fell from the monster's claws, from the person it took," said the third traveler, and the other two grew silent and solemn. The third villager pulled from his robe Zahra's mother's carrying sling, torn now, stained. He draped it gently across Zahra's lap, and inside Zahra found more sky-colored shards like those that had come from the egg, though these were wet and sticky and freshly broken. Spoiled golden yolk trickled out of the sling.

Zahra put her face into her hands and wept.

The travelers comforted her as best as they were able. They shared with her a little bag of dried meat and on her fire they heated a pot of couscous, pouring the precious grains through careful fingers. They fed her what they could spare, and some of what they could not. "Come with us," they said together, huddled around her hut's fire as night swept over the great grass sea. "Here it is so hot and so dry. The sun burns the life from everything. We are going to another country, Zahra, a place where it is not so hot and never so dry. A country where there is green everywhere."

Zahra, who did not know if green was a food or an animal or a kind of plant, shook her head.

"Zahra, please," the travelers said. "If you stay here alone, you will starve."

In her head Zahra heard the faint echo of her father's laughter. In her head Zahra heard her mother say, "A blessing. A gift."

She shook her head again, and though the travelers pleaded with her until the stars washed out of the sky, the next day they left her hut numbering still only three.

For days Zahra grieved. When she could be bothered to try for the sake of her begging belly, she attempted digging up more roots to gnaw. Sometimes she found them. Often she found only rocks. Eventually the blade of her hoe broke off its wooden handle, and she turned around and said, "Mama, how do I fix—" before remembering her mother was no longer there to answer her.

She cried. Not much: there was water to be had from a well near the hut's western wall, but it was hard for someone as weakened by hunger to turn the crank to bring the bucket up from the bottom. Sometimes Zahra was too dry inside to squeeze out even the smallest tears.

She grew hungrier and hungrier until the ache of her appetite kept her from sleeping, and that was a terrible, terrible thing. The worst thing, in fact, for only in dreams could she hope to see her mother again.

The moon grew in the sky night by night. When it was full at last, Zahra stepped out of her hut, her mother's tattered carrying sling around her neck. She looked out across the rippling grasses. She looked the direction the travelers had gone, with their dried meat and their couscous and their hopes of finding a green country. Then she looked in the direction her mother had gone, the way of sky-colored eggs and winged monsters that screeched and screamed and were big enough to block the sun.

She began to walk.

Near noon the next day, so weak she could barely stand, Zahra felt the ground go out from

beneath her feet. She stumbled and rolled down, down, down, scattering rocks and clay and empty seed pods, and she finally fetched up in a huge bowl-shaped pit hidden under the waving, rustling stalks of the great grass sea.

The pit was wide enough to have hidden her whole hut inside it. The floor of it was lined with soft dirt and a thick carpet of softer feathers: not a pit, then, but a nest.

Upside down on her back in the middle of the feathers, Zahra trembled. Her heart shuddered and quaked in her chest. "Wings," she croaked, remembering what the traveler had said. Bits of down flew from her lips and wafted away. "Wings that blocked the sun."

In the stippled half-darkness of the nest, something moved. A big something. A shadow fell over Zahra.

She looked up. A monster—the monster—looked back down at her, a winged beast greater in size than a cow, with gleaming golden eyes and a beak sharp as a skinning knife. That beak opened and it hissed at her, its tongue a narrow dart, its throat a horrible pink chasm. Zahra dug her heels into the soft feathery bottom of the nest and tried to push herself away from the beast, and it hissed at her again, a sound that raised the hair on the back of her neck, a sound that hurt her ears, a sound that—

A sound that was *words*. The beast was *talking*.

"Begone, pluckchild!" said the beast, and she scored the ground between Zahra's feet with curved, plated talons as yellow as the grass overhead. "Foul naked chick! Go! Get out of my nest or I'll eat you! I'll rip you to pieces! I'll—"

The beast's eyes found Zahra's torn carrying sling. Her pupils—dark slanted wells—narrowed to pinpoints. She arched her neck and dropped her head alongside Zahra's, her quilled breast heaving, her breath smelling of hot, hot wind and wet fetid meat. Her beak opened again. Zahra thought the beast would sink the hook of it through her heart, tear her open, take her life away.

Instead the beast hissed, "Want to steal my eggs, do you? Too bad, little pluckchild. They are gone, cracked and dead and done. I have no more."

And the beast withdrew in a boiling rush of feathers. She took herself to the far edge of the nest, where she tucked her wings over her face and pressed her beak into her forelegs, her golden eyes shut, her head bowed. She trembled as Zahra had trembled before, and a wrenching noise seeped from her throat, filling the nest, forcing Zahra to sit up and stare.

"Are you crying?" she asked the beast.

"My children were taken," the beast replied, and from her eyes trickled tears indeed. "Yes, foul chick, I am crying! My children—my eggs, yes, taken and broken and gone, both of them, by a horrible two-legged *thief*—"

"She wasn't horrible!" cried Zahra. She stood up and stomped over to the beast, though her strength was meager and her knees seesawed and wobbled. "She was wonderful and good and kind! She was my *mother*!"

The beast reared up over Zahra. Her feathers flared out in a quivering rainbow, shining reds and blues and purples like none Zahra had ever seen, and she screamed in a hoarse roaring snarl, "*She stole my children!*"

"To feed me!" Zahra screamed back. "She stole your eggs because I was starving and she wasn't horrible, she wasn't, she wasn't, she only wanted me not to be hungry *and you took her away from me!*"

Unable to stand anymore, Zahra sat down hard on the nest's carpet of feathers. She felt as dry inside as a fire must feel, and yet she hiccupped and choked and her sorrow came pouring out of her in a river of retching sobs. She wrapped her arms tight around herself. She shook and she shook, her belly a shrunken husk, her heart aching fit to burst.

The beast was still as long as it took Zahra to cry. She could have dispatched Zahra in one snap of her beak, maybe two, but instead she waited until Zahra had mostly quieted to say, her voice heavy and thick with a grief not unlike Zahra's own, "Why did you come here, pluckchild? To get revenge? To try to kill the creature that killed your mother? Is that it?"

"I don't know what *revenge* means," said Zahra miserably. "People... three people, they saw what you did to my mother. They told me. They said I should come with them to another country, a green country, but I don't know what *green* is either and they were nice but I didn't know them. I just know my mother's gone and she was all I had, and maybe your eggs were all you had and they're gone too, and I wondered..."

Zahra beat her dusty brown palms against her knees: once, twice. More tears oozed from the corners of her eyes. "I wondered," she said, "since I think you understand what it's like to lose everyone in the world you love, if maybe you might be able to tell me what I should do now."

Zahra looked up at the beast.

She said again, "What should I do now?"

The beast stared down at her in silence. Up close she was as beautiful as her eggs had been, the feathers of her face and neck and throat a riot of colors, her tawny pelt speckled and spotted and freckled. Her forelegs were a hawk's talons and yet her back feet were a lion's paws, and her tufted red tail swished through the feathers on the floor of the nest.

"Pluckchild," she said at last. "Do you have a name?"

"Zahra," said Zahra.

The beast studied her. Her red tail went swish, swish. Feathers drifted. The beast's eyes were wet. "Are you still hungry, Zahra?"

Zahra opened her mouth. Closed it. Her belly answered in her stead, groaning, and the beast snorted and huffed and rose. Her wings unfolded and flared, and with two mighty sweeps of them the beast was gone, sailing up and up out of the nest and through the grasses into the blue sky beyond, feathers fluttering everywhere.

For hours Zahra sat in the nest. She thought of leaving and going home, back to her hut, but when she tried to stand up her legs collapsed beneath her and delivered her to the ground.

The day dimmed. As the sun fell down into its slot on the horizon, the beast came flapping back into the nest. She landed by Zahra, shaking the ground, and from her talons she spilled into Zahra's lap a whole bushel of bright round red things, red as her tufted tail, red as the evening sky.

Mangoes.

"What do you think you should do now, little pluckchild?" said the beast, rending open the fruit with her claws. The scent of it was a bright tang in the gathering darkness, the sweet flesh a pale yellow like low, warm stars.

A gift, whispered her mother in Zahra's head. *Life.*

"I think I should eat," Zahra said, her mouth full of water. "It... may I eat? Mama, she—she would want me to eat. I want to. I want it."

The beast sighed. "Eat," she said, and as Zahra filled her belly the beast leaned in, closer and closer, looking at her from every side, and at last settled behind her, great spotted haunch tucked to Zahra's hip. With her beak she plucked feathers from Zahra's braids.

"I am sorry," the beast said at last, "that I took your mother away."

Her face and hands sticky with mango juice, Zahra said, "I'm sorry we took your eggs away too. Your babies." She closed her eyes. It was very dark behind the lids and her heartbeat thudded in her ears, and she said, feeling new tears slide down her face, "I'm so sorry. I am. But I'm angry too. At you! I'm so *angry* at you for what you did!"

"That is a feeling I share, pluckchild," said the beast, and in her haunch Zahra felt a quiver. "Yes, I am angry too. It is a very reasonable thing to be," and she sounded so like Zahra's mother that Zahra wept anew.

Neither of them moved from the other as night threw its purple shawl over the world. Feeling the slow, soft press of the beast's breath at her back, Zahra leaned little by little into a pillow of feathers and slept.

The next morning, after waking, Zahra made as though to climb out of the nest. When the beast stirred and asked her where she was going, Zahra said, "Home. I'm going home."

"At least eat first," said the beast in reply, and so Zahra did, and as juice dribbled down her chin she looked at the beast, full of anger, full of food, full of loss: fuller still of questions.

"What are you?" she asked, studying the beast's differing feet, her feathers, her tail.

"I am strong," said the beast. She stretched and flexed her wings. "My feathers are the sweeping clouds and the roar of the wind"—and she sounded very proud of herself, and she bobbed her head and somehow Zahra found a smile growing on her face, watching her—"and I am the furious scalding sun. Naked little pluckchildren like you call me a skylion."

"My mother used to tell me stories about magic creatures with names like that. Are you magic? Can you... can you make the sky do what you want?"

"No," said the skylion. "But the sky is my kingdom, and I can go anywhere in it that I wish to go."

Zahra looked around the nest, the mangoes both halved and whole: up, then, at the sky, flat and blue and going on forever. "How big is the sky?" she asked.

"Bigger than anything," said the skylion. "Bigger than everything. The sky... it wraps up the whole world, and the stars are in it like little seeds, and all those seeds hold every light and every color, and—"

The skylion said so many interesting things that Zahra could only listen until it grew dark again. She listened from one day to the next, and the next, and the day after that, over and over. She and the skylion talked together and they walked together, and though Zahra still missed her mother and longed to see her again, the hole in her heart that was her mother's absence did at least hurt a little less when the skylion fussed at her, or cleaned her braids, or told her stories, or tucked a wing over her at night to shield her from the mosquitoes and other biting insects.

One day—many, many days after she had found the nest in the first place—Zahra climbed from the nest and went back through the great grass sea until she came to the hut she had shared with her mother. The skylion made a looming shadow overhead. She watched Zahra touch the hut's walls, the little window, the crank of the well.

The skylion landed in the dooryard. Zahra went to her, wiping away tears, and the skylion said, "Do you wish for me to leave you here?"

"No," said Zahra. "No, please." She scrubbed her hands over her face. "Mama's gone," she said, "and I thought that meant everyone in the world I loved was gone, but then I found you. Please don't leave me." She clutched at the skylion's feathers and buried her face in them, and the skylion huffed and clicked her beak and arched her neck over Zahra, nipping soft at the space behind Zahra's ear where Zahra's mother had always pressed a loving thumb.

"No," the skylion. "No, little Zahra, little chick. No, I won't leave you."

They looked at the sky together, then, the sweeping blue bowl of it. "Can we go to the green country?" asked Zahra. "Somewhere new and good?" And what she meant was somewhere without torn slings or shattered shells. Zahra said, "You said the sky wraps up the whole world. Let's go see it. Let's go see green."

The skylion cast her gaze over the waves of the great grass sea, the yellow stalks, the hard broken ground, the rocks jutting up like cruel blunt teeth. Zahra's fingers slid through her feathers.

"Yes," said the skylion, turning into her touch. "Yes, my chick. Let's go."

Zahra clambered up behind her wings and held tight to her, and they flew up, up, up into the sky. They climbed the clouds, and anyone watching them would have seen them grow smaller and smaller until they were but another flicker of heat dancing on the horizon, the only thing left of either of them a whisper of laughter and a few fluttering feathers.

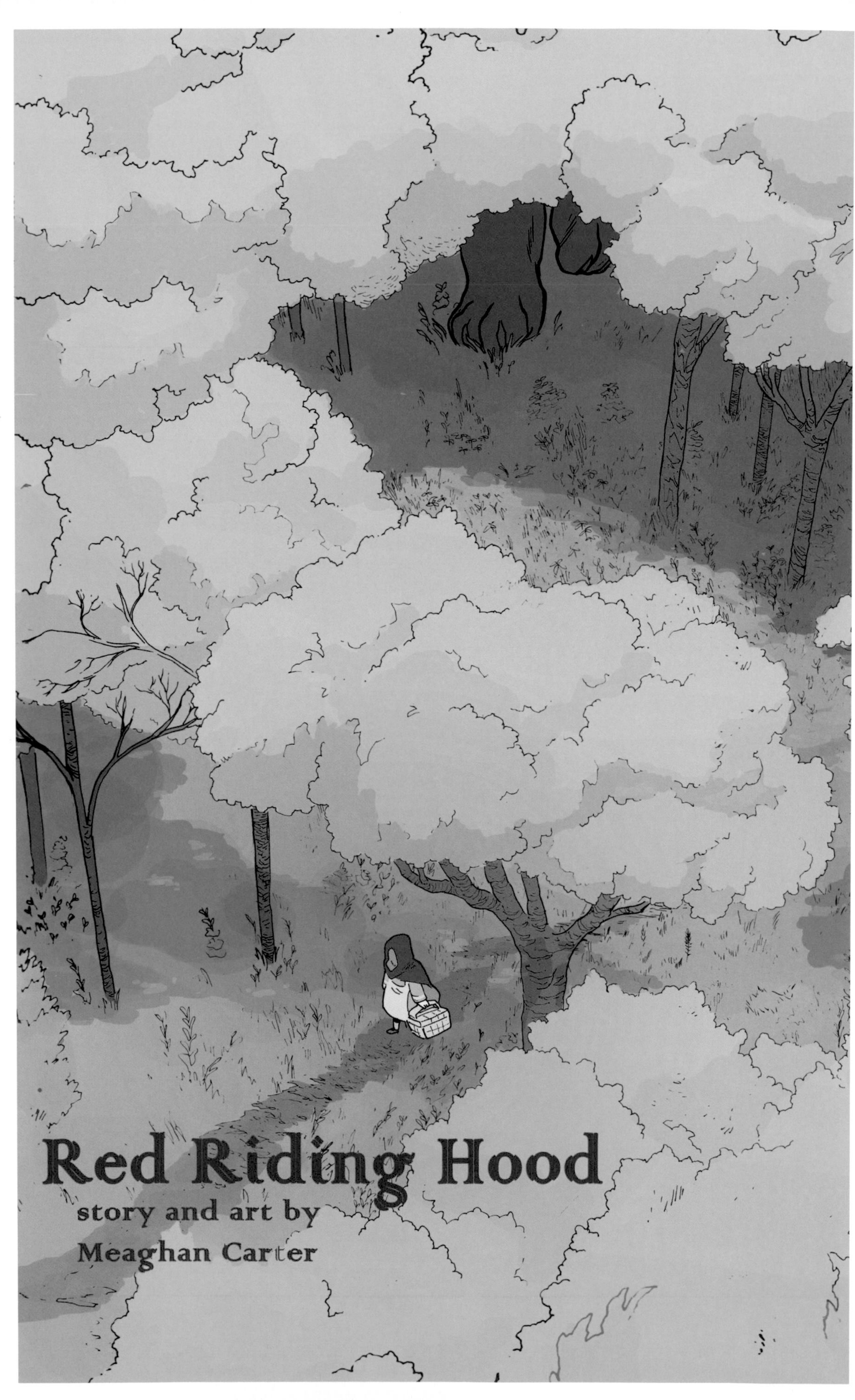
Red Riding Hood
story and art by
Meaghan Carter

I want to see you happy, child.
I want to see you grow.

Let your dreams
climb mountains

Find flowers

and gather snow.

Run wild in fields of poppies

Run while you still can, child
Before the dark rings midnight's bell.

If the dark does find you, child
Before you make it home
Then I hope it finds you happy
Then I hope it finds you happy

Don't fear the hand of dark, my child
Follow his midnight bell.
Because the dark comes for all of us
Even in beds of asphodel.

East Of The Sun
West Of The Moon
-BY MORGAN BEEM

CHILD. WHY HAVE
YOU COME?

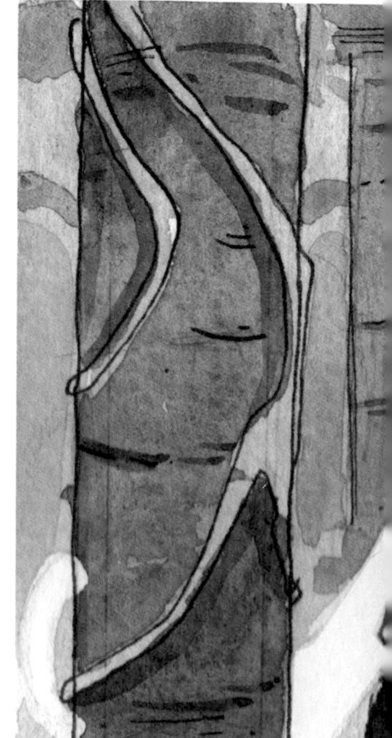

ALL THE WAY
TO THE TEMPLE
OF THE GREAT WIND?

SPIRIT OF THE WIND,
FIRST, ALLOW ME TO TELL
YOU MY STORY...

ONE NIGHT, THE BEAR CAME FOR ME.
IF I WENT,
HE PROMISED TO MAKE MY FAMILY WEALTHY IN RETURN.
I AGREED, AND WE JOURNEYED TO HIS CASTLE.
WE LIVED HAPPILY.

BUT EVERY NIGHT, THE BEAR TURNED INTO A MAN.
I ONLY WANTED TO SEE HIM.
TO KNOW HE WASN'T A MONSTER.
BUT HE WAS SO BEAUTIFUL.
I LOOKED TOO LONG.

I HAD FAILED, HE EXPLAINED.
IF ONLY I HAD BEEN PATIENT A LITTLE LONGER.

AND NOT LOOKED AT HIM, HIS CURSE WOULD HAVE BEEN BROKEN.

BUT NOW HE HAD TO GO,

TO THE PALACE THAT WAS EAST OF THE SUN AND WEST OF THE MOON.
TO MARRY THE TROLL QUEEN.

I GRIEVED.

AND THEN I KNEW WHAT I HAD TO DO.

AND THAT IS WHY
I CAME TO YOU.

ONLY YOU, GREAT NORTH WIND...

CAN CARRY ME EAST OF THE
SUN, AND WEST OF THE MOON.

SO I CAN STOP THE TROLL
QUEEN'S WEDDING,

AND WIN BACK
MY LOVE.

BY NICOLE CHARTRAND

ADAPTED FROM HANS CHRISTIAN ANDERSON'S "THE WILD SWANS"

WHEN I WAS A CHILD, MY MOTHER FELL ILL AND DIED. MY FATHER, A WEALTHY MERCHANT, SOON REMARRIED, SEDUCED BY A WITCH WHO POISONED HIS MIND AND BODY UNTIL HE WAS NO MORE THAN A PUPPET. SHE THEN BEGAN TRYING TO MANIPULATE HIS CHILDREN IN TURN.
WE KNEW WHAT SHE'D DONE AND WE WOULDN'T GIVE IN. THUS, THE DAY BEFORE MY ELDEST BROTHER CAME OF AGE, SHE TURNED HER MAGIC UPON US. WHILE I SOMEHOW MANAGED TO HIDE FROM HER, MY SEVEN BROTHERS WERE NOT SO LUCKY. DOWN TO THE LAST, THE WITCH CHANGED THEM INTO SWANS AND LOCKED THEM AWAY.
AFRAID SHE'D ATTACK ME NEXT, I FREED MY BROTHERS FROM THEIR CAGES AND WE MADE OUR ESCAPE, TAKING FLIGHT IN THE VAIN HOPE WE MIGHT OUTRUN THE REACH OF HER CURSE. I PROMISED I WOULD FIND A WAY TO SAVE THEM. BUT WITH EVERY PASSING MONTH WE SEARCHED, MY HOPE OF KEEPING THAT PROMISE FADED A LITTLE MORE.

THEN, IN A CITY ON A HILL BY THE OCEAN, WHEN MY WEARY BROTHERS COULD CARRY ME NO LONGER, I FOUND A WAY TO HELP THEM AT LAST.

COME NEAR, CHILD. YOU ARE THE ONE THEY CALL ELISE?
Y-YES.

I AM QUEEN TO THE FAIRIES OF THIS LAND. MY SUBJECTS HAVE SPOKEN OF YOUR PLIGHT.
YOU HOLD WITHIN YOURSELF THE POWER TO BREAK THE CURSE ON YOUR BROTHERS, ALTHOUGH IT WILL NOT BE A SIMPLE TASK.

IF YOU WISH TO HELP THEM, YOUR PATH STARTS IN THIS VERY GRAVEYARD, WHERE THE STINGING NETTLES GROW BESIDE THE TOMBS.
YOU MUST PLUCK THEM WITH YOUR BARE HANDS AND CRUSH THEM INTO INK WITH YOUR BARE FEET.
WITH THE INK AND A QUILL FROM A BROTHER'S WING, INSCRIBE A SPELL OF MY MAKING UPON YOUR SKIN.
COMPLETE IT BEFORE THE FIRST DAWN OF AUTUMN.
ON THAT DAY, STAND ATOP THE SPIRIT STONES OF THE EASTERN CLIFFS, WHERE THE FIRST RAYS OF SUNLIGHT WILL BREAK THE CURSE WITH THEIR TOUCH.
BE WARNED: ONCE YOU BEGIN, YOUR WORDS AND YOUR BROTHERS' LIVES WILL BE WOVEN INTO THE INSCRIPTION.
ONLY THE SPELL WILL POUR FORTH IF YOU TRY TO WRITE, AND YOU MUST NOT SPEAK UNTIL THE CURSE IS BROKEN,
FOR ANY WORDS THAT FALL FROM YOUR LIPS WILL BE THOSE OF THE SPELL. AND THEY WILL LAND LIKE DAGGERS IN YOUR BROTHERS' HEARTS. NOW, DO YOU STILL WANT TO HELP THEM?
YES. I'LL DO IT.

VERY WELL.
I SHALL GIVE YOU THE WORDS OF THE INSCRIPTION. USE THEM WISELY, ELISE.

WHEN I SAT DOWN TO WRITE, THE ENCHANTED INK BURNED LIKE FIRE AS SYMBOLS AND WORDS LEAPT FROM THE QUILL ONTO MY SKIN, AS IF THE SPELL HAD A WILL OF ITS OWN AND WAS FIGHTING MINE.

MY BROTHERS BROUGHT ME FOOD AND WATER AND TRIED TO KEEP ME IN GOOD SPIRITS.

I WORKED IN SILENCE, ALONE SAVE FOR SWANS AND STINGING NETTLES. I KNEW THE ROAD THAT LAY AHEAD WOULD BE DIFFICULT AND LONELY.

AND IT WAS, FOR A WHILE.

UNTIL ONE DAY, SOMEONE BROKE THE SILENCE.

HE TOLD ME HIS NAME, BUT ONLY LATER DID HE REVEAL HE WAS TO BE CROWNED KING.

WHY DO THEY ONLY LIKE YOU?! OW!!
I MUST ADMIT, I DIDN'T BELIEVE HIM AT ALL.

YET NO MATTER WHO HE REALLY WAS OR WASN'T, I WAS ALWAYS HAPPY TO SEE HIM WHEN HE'D VISIT.

HE WAS NEVER AFRAID, AND ALWAYS RETURNED TO KEEP ME COMPANY AS I WORKED TO SAVE MY BROTHERS.

WITH LITTLE TIME TO SPARE BEFORE FALL,

I MANAGED TO COMPLETE THE FAIRY QUEEN'S INSCRIPTION.

UNCLE?

...FAR BE IT FROM ME TO TELL MY KING HOW TO LIVE HIS LIFE--
--BUT I'D LIKE TO KNOW WHY HIS MAJESTY SPENDS SO MUCH TIME IN THAT GRAVEYARD WITH A VILE SORCERESS.

MISS?!
THERE YOU ARE! I NEED TO WARN YOU!

THE REGENT, MY UNCLE, HAS BEEN SPYING ON US, ON YOU!
HE'S CONVINCED THAT YOU'RE SOME KIND OF WITCH!
HE HAS GUARDS WITH HIM TONIGHT, AND THEY'RE ON THEIR WAY HERE.
I'M AFRAID HE MIGHT TRY TO KILL YOU!

I-I'M SO SORRY.
THIS IS ALL BECAUSE OF ME. I--

NO, WAIT, PLEASE!
I WISHED TO BE ABLE TO TELL HIM WHAT I HAD TO DO.
YET I COULD ONLY RUN TOWARD THE CLIFFS THROUGH THE NIGHT.

THE RING OF STONES WAS THERE, JUST AS THE FAIRY HAD TOLD ME IT WOULD BE.

BUT I HAD RUN OUT OF TIME.

NOTHING TO SAY IN YOUR OWN DEFENSE!?
THIS IS YOUR LAST CHANCE, WITCH.

SO BE IT. GUARDS--

NO--STOP!!!

UNCLE, STOP THIS AT ONCE!
THIS IS INSANE! SHE'S DONE ME NO HARM!
I DON'T KNOW EXACTLY WHAT SHE IS, BUT I'M CERTAIN IT'S NOT A WITCH!

BESOTTED BOY! CAN'T YOU SEE SHE HAS YOU UNDER THE POWER OF HER SPELLS?!
IF YOU WON'T COME TO YOUR SENSES ON YOUR OWN, THEN I'LL BE THE ONE TO PUT AN END TO THIS!
MEN! KILL THE W--
BRONK!

HONK!
--WHA--?!
HONK!
HONK!
BRONK!
GASP

BUT THEY'RE HUMAN AGAIN... IT'S OVER!

LET OUR SISTER GO FREE!

SHE'S THE ONE WHO SAVED US!

WE WON'T LET YOU HARM HER.

YOUR MAJESTY, I... THE SPELL THAT BOUND MY BROTHERS AND I FOR SO LONG IS BROKEN.

...WE'RE FINALLY FREE.

PLEASE

by August & Cory Brown

Once upon a time, there were two sisters. They lived in a cold and wintry kingdom, whose people toiled to survive while their King feasted and was merry.
Rose Red was a bold huntress and a skilled trapper.
Snow White was an accomplished herbalist, wise and learned in many things.
Together, they lived well, in spite of the howling winter winds.

THUMP
THUD
One cold night, there was a knock at their door.

To their surprise, a wounded bear stood at the threshold, a sword thrust into its back.
PLEASE

After a moment's indecision, they invited the odd guest to come inside.

The beast settled by the hearth at once.
The sisters decided that one of them would always be awake to watch it, and to keep the fire stoked.
But the night was long, and their eyes were weary.
So they slept.

In the morning, the sisters found the bear curled up alongside them.

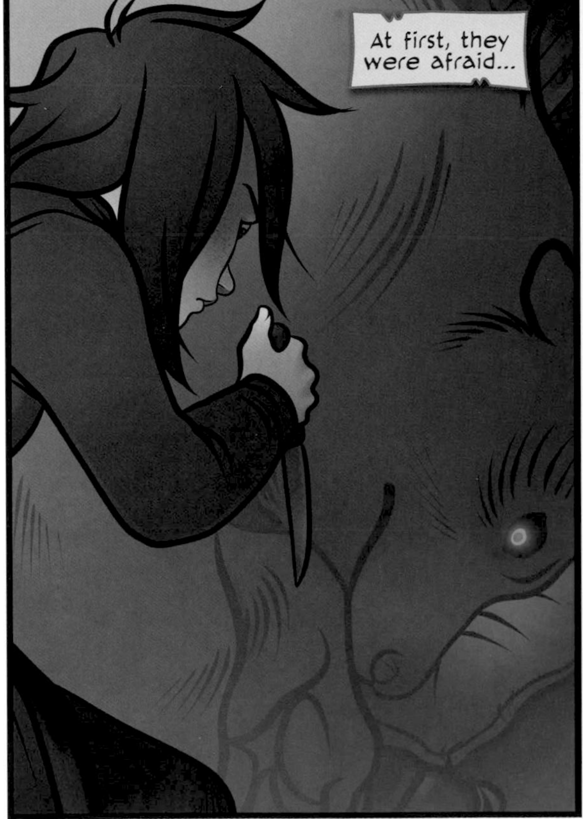

They shared their meal with their guest.

Snow White felt badly for the wounded creature, and made to remove the sword from its side.

But the bear drew away, growling, as she reached for the blade.

So Snow White let it be.

When it had eaten, the bear departed as suddenly as it came, leaving the sisters to wonder.

For the next week, the bear returned every night, and the three of them slept by the hearth.
Every morning, it would share a meal with its gracious hostesses, then leave. They began to look forward to their strange friend's visits.
The girls went about their lives as usual, though curiosity tormented them.
KNOCK KNOCK
They were surprised to hear a knock at their door during the daytime.
They were even more surprised when their visitor was not the bear, but the King!

The King told them that he was hunting a fearsome beast. He spoke of a great bear which, in its murderous hunger, had already slain his younger brother.
Though the King had lodged his finest sword in the monster's back, it had escaped him.
He asked the sisters if they had seen the creature, and promised a reward if they led him to his vengeance.
Snow White and Rose Red looked at one another.
Both knew that his claims could not be true. So they lied to the King.
The King thanked them for hearing his tale, and went on his way.

But the King recognized their deception. That night, he returned alone, and watched their cabin in secret.

The moment the bear had found its spot by the fire, the King burst triumphantly through the door, blade in hand.

They pleaded with the King to spare the bear. Such a gentle creature could not be his brother's killer.

But he only laughed, and mockingly congratulated them for their wisdom.

The arrogant King boasted of his cunning.
He had invited his brother to hunt, and struck him with a cursed sword meant to turn him into a beast.
Though the King had missed his mark, he could still blame the bear for his brother's death...
...and when he brought back its head, no one would suspect that he, himself, was the slayer of the only other heir to the throne.
His power would be absolute.
NO! PLEASE

As the gloating King readied his blade, he promised to commission a memorial for the sisters... and mount it alongside the head of the bear that killed them.
Though unarmed, Rose Red damned the King for a coward, and readied herself to fight.
The bear drew near, and spoke one last request.
PLEASE
When Rose drew out the cursed blade, the bear collapsed in a pool of blood.

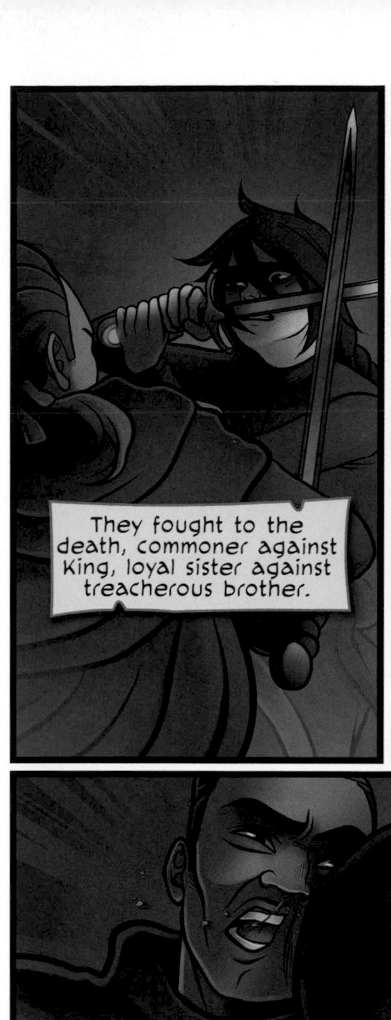

They fought to the death, commoner against King, loyal sister against treacherous brother.

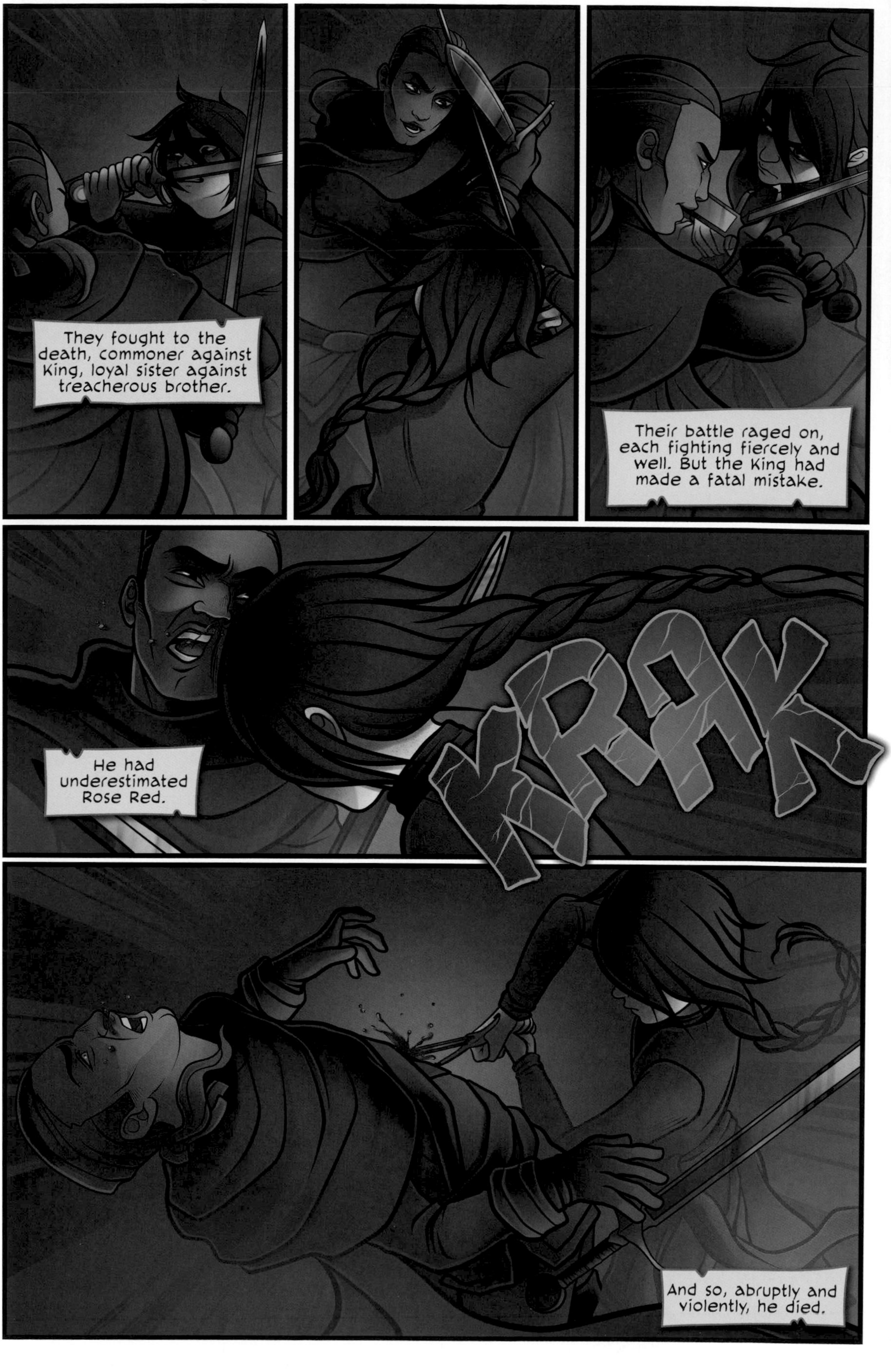

Their battle raged on, each fighting fiercely and well. But the King had made a fatal mistake.

He had underestimated Rose Red.

KRAK

And so, abruptly and violently, he died.

With the death of its master, the sword's curse was broken. The last heir to the throne, newly restored to his true form, lay bleeding to death on the floor.
The dying prince thanked the sisters for their kindness, and for avenging him before his passing.
Snow White interrupted his self-pity to gently remind him that she was an expert healer.

After resting the night under Snow White's watchful eye, the ragged prince gathered the strength to set out.

Uniting with his brother's hunting party, he shared his tale with them, and was brought safely home.

He was soon crowned King, and his reign was humble and kind.

And his people prospered.

For their part, Snow White and Rose Red lived on as they always had.

TAP TAP
One cold night, there was a knock at their door.

To their surprise, an old friend stood at the threshold.

Please?
END.

All Furs

Story by Joanne Webster
Art by Emily Hann

The glow of the morning sun barely pierced the thick foliage of the dark forest. Many feared these woods, but I loved them. It was a bountiful hunting ground. By mid afternoon, my men and I had caught six large pheasants and one deer.

"When should we head back, your Highness?" asked Sir Richard, my father's oldest knight, as I inspected my arrows.

"Let's see if we can catch one more deer," I replied playfully, much to Sir Richard's annoyance. He's rather determined to protect me, the sole heir to the throne. I do enjoy testing to see how many grey hairs I could give him every once in a while. "Then we'll return-"

Something furry caught my eye as it passed behind a large oak. I spurred my horse forward in a mild gallop. The creature was slow and oddly shaped. I prepared my bow. My first assumption was that it was a bear, as it was too small and too arched to be a deer. The animal turned towards me, revealing what looked like the flattened face of a donkey covered with other skins. The creature moved back, tripped and gave a loud "Eeep!" as it fell over a log.

I halted my horse and lowered my bow. It would be impossible for me to miss my target at this range, but since in my experience, animals don't cry out "Eeep!" when they fall, I was beginning to worry I had stumbled upon a fairy or troll of some sort. The many disturbing tales my father had told me as a child of magical beasts populating this forest echoed in my mind. "You! Identify yourself!" I said. "I am the Crown Princess Avery, so if you try-"

"Don't shoot!" A dirt-covered hand appeared from behind the log. "I mean no harm!"

It was a girl's voice. She stood up, revealing a rather astonishing appearance. The girl was covered head to toe in furs. It was nothing like a typical fur coat. It seemed to be sewn together from every kind of pelt imaginable. There was a bear skin covering her head and fox and wolf pelts dangling off her shoulders. Feathers and weasel husks hung off her waist as a long skirt with the hem stopping above her ankles. There were other furs mixed within the coat that I didn't recognize, many with spots and stripes, quite possibly from animals not found in my country.

I could barely make out the girl's face from beneath the bear pelt as it too was covered in dirt. She looked as if she was trying to vanish into the mixed layers of her coat.

"Who?" I stammered, baffled, "or what are you?"

"I-I am All Furs," she said in a hoarse voice, as if she hadn't spoken in months. "I am a wayward orphan with no home to call her own. Please have pity on me or a curse will fall upon you."

I raised an eyebrow. "The Story of the Queen Mary and the Hunter."

The girl lifted her head. "Pardon?"

"That line you just said is from the play, The Story of the Queen Mary and the Hunter," I repeated, amused. This girl certainly was an odd one. That wasn't even one of the better lines in the play. The girl tilted her head and then sighed. "Darn, I was hoping that would convince you to leave me alone."

"You thought you could fool me with a line from a play?"

"It's not exactly a well known play," she responded and I couldn't deny that. Not many people had heard of it outside Troila. I only happen to know it due to my love of the theater. "Give me another hour, and I can think of something more clever," she insisted with great conviction.

I tried to suppress the laughter that wanted to escape my throat. "Is your name really All Furs?"

"Yes," said the girl, "and I truly do live in these woods."

I frowned as I glanced around. She sounded barely older than me. "It's a rather dangerous place for a person to live in. There are bears, wild boars and I've heard trolls roam here too."

All Furs gave a shrug as I heard the knights catching up to me. "There are far worse things than worrying if a bear or a troll will eat you."

Before I could reply, I saw Sir Richard ready his bow at the girl, but I raised my arm to stop him. "It's alright, she's just a girl who steals lines from plays."

"I wasn't stealing! I was borrowing," All Furs replied, sharply.

The knights stared in confusion at each other as I looked back to All Furs. "Why were you running from us?"

"Why?" All Furs said as she held up her arms showing off more of her coat. "Because you are hunters, and I am nothing but all furs. I was certain you would mistake me for an animal and stick an arrow in my back."

"Fair point," I said as I nudged my horse to step forward. I offered my hand to All Furs. "If you come with us to the palace, you wouldn't have to worry about any of those things."

All Furs stared at my hand and shyly poked at it like she expected it to dissolve. "You would let me live at the palace?"

"Yes," I said. "Surely, the cook or someone can find work for you to do."

"Princess," Sir Richard said as he looked at All Furs suspiciously. "I'm not sure your mother would approve of this."

"It's hardly the first or last thing I would do that she hated," I grumbled back as I kept my hand out to All Furs. "So, what do you say? Would you like to come with us, fair maiden?"

All Furs remained quiet, staring sternly at me, as if she was trying to read my mind. For a second, I thought she was going to run off and disappear in the dark forest, but she gingerly took my hand. "All right, if you insist."

I pulled her up onto my horse, and I felt her small hands wrap around my waist. "Right, men! Let's go home!" I called to them as my horse turned to gallop. "We'll continue the hunt tomorrow. Who knows what we'll find then." I looked back to All Furs as we rode, hoping to catch a glance of her face, but she kept her face turned downward and hidden from me as we returned to the palace.

As fully expected, my mother was less than thrilled when I presented All Furs to her. However, she agreed with me that it wouldn't be right to let a girl live in the forest all on her own. After much discussion and assurance to the horrified cook that All Furs would not

leave hairs in her food, we assigned All Furs to the kitchen.

I had wanted to give her a bed in the servant quarters, but our servants refused and my mother agreed. Seemed none of the servants enjoyed the idea of sharing their quarters with a strange wild person from the woods "Heaven knows what she has crawling in there!" the maids complained.

"And we don't want to wake up to find our beds crawling with fleas," exclaimed the footmen. "We have our health to think of here! It's hard enough to keep the place clean as is."

Mother then suggested All Furs may be more content to sleep in the stables where she would have more privacy.

"Switching from living in isolation to being surrounded by a crowd does take time to adjust," my mother argued. I was still strongly against it, but All Furs accepted it with no fuss. According to her, living in the stables was a luxury after surviving in the woods for so long.

"Besides," All Furs said, "your mother is correct. It's a little overwhelming. It would be nice to have a little solitude." I was still reluctant, but there wasn't much I could do if All Furs was fine with it, so I had no choice but to accept it.

I didn't see All Furs again until later that evening as the seamstress was finishing my fitting for my ballgown. She was carrying a pile of logs in her arms.

"I was asked to bring wood for your fire," All Furs said as she started to retreat. "But I can come back later."

"No, it's fine. We were done anyway," I replied as the seamstress collected my dress and gave a curtsy before exiting the room. I then went to sit in my chair to check that none of the heads of my arrows were loose as I watched All Furs go to the fireplace.

"Is it alright if I call you 'Furs'?" I asked.

"If you wish," All Furs said with a shrug. "My name doesn't mean much to me. May I ask what the gown was for?"

I sighed. "It's for the Winter Balls next month," I said, grumbling. "All three of them."

"You have three balls?" she asked surprised.

"Tradition," I said with a shrug. "It's supposedly a way for me to find the best person for me to marry. I don't mind the dancing," I leaned back into the chair ,"but I'm not looking forward to my mother's nagging on which prince or princess I should be dancing with."

She gave me a half smile. "It is a nice dress at least, I haven't worn one in years."

"I could find you some new clothes if you like," I offered. "I know the cook will be overworking you for the ball, so you should get some reward for that."

All Furs chuckled and shook her head, causing the fox and wolf tails to quiver on her shoulders. "No, it's fine, this coat is all I need."

"Have you always lived in the woods?" I couldn't believe she had. Her manner of speaking

combined with her knowledge of the arts implied that Furs must have been in a city at some point. It wasn't as if plays were often performed in the middle of a woods by rabbits.

Furs remained quiet as she dumped more logs into the fireplace. I thought she hadn't heard me, but then she softly said, "I used to live in the country of Trolia, but not anymore."

"Trolia?" I replied surprised. I had thought she wasn't a local, but I never would have guessed she'd come from a country far over the mountain range. "I did hear a lot of people fled Trolia during the last few years of King Louis's reign, but from there to here? That's a long trip."

Furs paused as she turned to look at me. "King Louis reigns no more?"

I gave a nod as I placed my arrows with the others. "His nephew is king now. Good thing too. I heard King Louis went quite insane when his wife passed away. He almost brought the kingdom to ruin with his irrational wars and ludicrous declarations. Rumor has it, he was planning to marry his own daughter." She winced at those words. Clearly, she had experienced first hand the problems of the kingdom. I pretended to ignore it, not wishing to embarrass her with questions. If Furs had to flee Trolia and forced to live in a forest to feel safe, she probably wasn't eager to discuss it. "I just hope that the nephew will be more stable, and the country can fully recover and start anew with their old king dead."

Furs then jumped to her feet, shaking. "Dead?"

I looked at her curiously. "You haven't heard?" It was all anyone had talked about when it happened, but who knew how long Furs had been living in the woods by herself. "King Louis passed away two years ago." They had claimed it was sickness, although many believed that someone had slipped a little something extra into the King's supper the night before he passed.

Furs shuddered, wrapping her tattered fur coat tighter around herself. "He's dead. He's truly dead," she muttered.

"Are you okay?" I asked, as I reached out to touch her shoulder.

Furs took a breath and held her head high. "Yes, I'm fine." She gave a swift bow. "Do you need anything else of me tonight?"

I pressed my lips together, wishing to find another topic to so I could keep talking with her, but found myself dismissing her . "No, thank you, Furs," I said and gestured to the door. "Why don't you go rest. I'll see you tomorrow."

She gave a nod before creeping out of the room, meekly as a mouse. I sat and stared into the fire as my brain pondered what Furs had said.

The next month flew by. Both my parents were running around like headless chickens as the date of the first ball approached. I tried to see Furs when I could, but my chances were limited thanks to the added sword, manner and dance lessons my mother crammed into my schedule. It was only when Furs would come into my room each night to tend to the fire that I had a few blissful moments with her. We talked of various topics; recipes, novels, castle life, sewing, what berries to eat and not eat while in the woods if you didn't wish to be poisoned. Truthfully, I was becoming quite fond of her, and I grew more curious about where my furry friend originally come from. Each time I tried to approach the subject, Furs would hastily change it. It was clear she didn't wish to discuss it. Eventually, I decided to let Furs keep her secrets, at least for now.

The night of the Winter Ball came. My parents debated which outfit I should be wearing for the first dance; the gown or the military tunic. I had hoped I could slip Furs out of the kitchen so she could steal a glimpse of the party, but I was unable to escape the unending line of guests I had to greet.

As the line was finally shorter, the orchestra began the first notes of the ball's opening dance, a lively tune meant to energize the crowd. As the guests flocked towards me, all eager to be my first dance partner, I knew it was impossible for me to leave without being impolite.

I danced with five princes and four princesses, and they were pleasant enough, but their attempts at small talk made me uncomfortable. One can only discuss the current weather a certain number of times and I wasn't at all interested in the Prince of Romana's fascination with agricultural history and ancient pottery. After the fifth princess and I ended our dance, I went to get a much-needed drink. My mother glided towards me, smiling. "There are many wonderful suitors for you to choose from."

"Yes, mother. I know," I replied dryly.

"Don't slouch, dear. A future ruler needs good posture."

I sighed, half expecting her to start fixing my hair.

The familiar voice of the sentry at the door resonated as he, as always, announced a new guest. But this time, his voice cracked unexpectedly. The crowd turned to see who had shocked him so, as the sentry was rarely astonished. A few guests gasped, taken aback by the vision that stepped through the doorway. "Who is that girl?" my mother asked, stunned. "I've never seen her before."

The girl spotted me and made a beeline towards me, weaving through the flock of princesses assembled before me. The best word to describe her would have been "glowing". She had long flowing golden hair that mixed with the design of her gown, made of a material that shone as brightly as the sun itself. She was dazzling to say the least.

My mother stepped aside with a sly smile as the girl approached and bowed. I noticed then her eyes were brown, gentle and kind, like those of a deer. I could have sworn I had seen those same eyes before. She had tiny freckles decorating her nose and cheeks.

"May I have this dance, Princess Avery?" she asked.

I nearly choked on my drink as I gulped it down. "Um...er...yes...what's your name?"

She smiled sweetly at me as she offered her hand. "You may call me Samantha, or Sam for short."

We drifted to the dance floor. She twirled and glided effortlessly, as if she was weightless, like sunlight. She barely casted a shadow, she seemed like a dream.

"Y-you are a good dancer," I complimented, overwhelmed.

"As are you," Sam commented, amused by my enthusiasm.

Sam and I danced together for the next hour. I found myself talking to her in a way I had never spoken with anyone else before... Except maybe Furs. Oddly enough, faced with such a vision, I kept thinking back to my friend in the kitchens. The orchestra took a short

break, allowing the guests to mingle. I turned away for a moment, to answer the Prince of Romana's insistent questions, only to find her gone.

No one seemed to know where Sam had come from or when she had come. She had appeared and vanished through the door, as if it was enchanted. The ball ended soon after her departure. I tried my best to be a good host, but my mind kept drifting back to Sam. All I could do was hope she would return for the next ball.

My parents hounded me with questions about the mysterious princess. They were as smitten as I was. Sam was the talk of the castle. Everyone was sharing tales about the Sunlight Princess.

A few days before the second ball, I sighed wistfully as I prepared for bed when I heard a knock at the door.

"Princess Avery," the cook called. "I have some bread soup for you."

I had been so busy dancing and daydreaming I hadn't been able to eat much. "Bring it in."

The cook came in and set the tray on the table as I finished brushing my hair. The cook watched me, strangely anxious. She usually stayed to ensure the meal tasted fine, but so far, she had never disappointed me. Why was she so nervous?

I dipped my spoon in and took a mouthful. The taste surprised me. The cook's bread soup wasn't bad, but I had always found it too salty. This bread soup, however, was perfect. I raised an eyebrow at the cook who coughed uncomfortably as I continued to eat my meal. I enjoyed every delicious mouthful until I got to the last few spoonfuls. It was then that I saw something glitter at the bottom of the bowl and fished it out with my spoon.

It was a solid gold ring. I knew the cook didn't own such fine jewellery, and even if she did, she wasn't so careless as to leave it in a soup.

"Who made this?" I asked, as I slipped the gold ring into my pocket without the cook seeing. "I know it wasn't you."

"It does taste bad doesn't it? I knew it!" The cook exclaimed as if she had been expecting this to happen. "I didn't make it, It was All Furs."

"Furs?" I said, astonished. I didn't know she could cook this well. I paused, thinking back on the past weeks. I barely spoke to her, consumed by my curiosity of Sam. I spent weeks being selfish while my friend must have been practicing her culinary skills to surprise me. I felt awful.

"Forgive me, your Highness but I was busy helping the sous-chef, and All Furs offered to make the soup for me. She insisted, but if I had known it would turn out this horrible-"

"It's fine," I said as I raised my hand to hush her rambling. "Please send her up."

The cook looked confused, but relieved. She took my tray and left. I didn't have to wait long for Furs to appear.

"What may I do for your Highness?" she asked.

I held up the gold ring to her. "I found this in the soup, is it yours?"

Furs shook her head. "No, it is not."

I frowned as I fiddled with the ring. "Do you know how it got there?"

She shrugged. "I do not, but perhaps someone slipped it in when I wasn't looking."

I could not see that being likely. Who would willingly put treasure in a soup? "Is that all, Princess Avery?" Furs asked dryly as she tucked her hands into the sleeves of her coat.

"It is, thank you," I replied, a bit upset my friend seemed unwilling to speak to me. I watched her leave as I continued to fiddle with the gold ring. I wondered if it would fit perfectly on Furs's slim fingers.

The next ball came and I felt excited. I was dying to see Sam again, but as the night grew shorter, I worried she would not appear. Close to midnight, the sentry announced her. This time, his voice was booming and enchanted. The guests giggled and whispered, thrilled to see the mysterious princess once more.

She wore a different dress, this one was a dark and deep blue, spotted with specks of silver that shimmered and converged in a moon symbol that seemed to be waning as she moved. A silver pin held her hair up, the color of which seemed clouded, to match the nighttime color of the gown.

I practically ran towards her, asking her for a dance when she had barely made it through the doorway. She smiled at me adorably, mouthing, "Yes". Her freckles had been decorated with small glitters that made her skin look like it was alight with constellations.

Once again, I felt at ease talking to Sam. I learned she loved cooking, but she also enjoyed needlework and had been curious to learn about archery.

"I could teach you," I offered as we twirled along to the music. "I'm quite a good shot."

"Oh, I know," she said with a sly smile. "You're handy to have in a hunt."

I was curious to ask just how she could know that when the music stopped. Again, all it took was a short distraction and she was gone.

I was disappointed, but I wasn't as discouraged as after the previous ball since I had a better sense that I would see her again. The third ball still remained. And this time, I'd keep hold of her hand.

The next night, as every night, the cook brought me bread soup, and as I got to the last spoonful, I found a tiny golden spinning wheel. The cook stared aghast as I caught the trinket in my spoon. She confirmed it was Furs who had made the soup and fetched her for me. Furs stepped in and I held up the spinning wheel for her to see.

"Is this yours?" I asked.

"No," she replied with a smile. "That does not look like something I would own."

I drummed my fingers against my knee as I tried to decipher her expression. "Why do you think," I inquired, "that these little trinkets only seem to appear after you deliver my soup?"

"I do not know, your Highness," All Furs replied.

"These aren't jewels anyone would have," I said as I toyed with the spinning wheel in my hand. "I've heard these are common Christening gifts given to royal children. So, why would they be appearing in my soup?"

"I do not know," Furs said. "Perhaps your gifts are late and a fairy saw to correct it."

I stared at her, unconvinced. "Furs, do you like dancing?"

She winced slightly, but she kept her rigid smile. "I can't say I've had much practice in the woods, so I doubt I would be a good dance partner." She ducked her face in farther under her fur hood. "Is that all, Princess Avery?"

"Yes, thank you," I muttered and watched her leave. I had a theory on Furs's identity, but I needed solid proof. The next morning, I summoned to my chambers the conductor of the orchestra. I had a secret request for him and his musicians.

The next ball came, I fidgeted with the gold ring in my pocket and patted it for luck when Sam appeared.

The dress she was wearing was my favourite among the three. It reminded me of the dim woods where I had found Furs. It was a dark pine green, and was layered with lace as delicate as rose petals and as detailed as leaves. The hem seemed to move like leaves carried by the wind. Her hair looked almost brown against the woodland gown and was held up by twigs and vines fashioned into a tiara. More than ever, her kind eyes reminded me of a doe.

I walked towards her, confident as ever, and invited her to dance. Our routine repeated and we chatted as usual. Sam seemed to think nothing was amiss as we discussed whether you could shoot an apple off a person's head, when suddenly she frowned. I knew she had expected the music to end, but the musicians continued to play, just as I had asked them to. Another group of musicians was ready to step in whenever some of the players needed a break. Sam was getting anxious. She stumbled and her fingers on my shoulder grew tense.

Sam wanted to flee, but I kept a hold on her arm. "Come," I said with a smile. "I want you to meet my parents."

Her eyes widened, and she shook her head. "No, I'm sorry, but I have to go."

"But it's only polite," I locked eyes with her and slipped the golden ring onto her finger.

"No, I am so sorry, Avery," she pleaded, "but I can't." She yanked her arm free, and I let her go. I resisted chasing after her as she fled. The ball ended soon afterward, and I was still in my dress when the cook came to bring me my soup.

"Oh, sorry, your Highness," the cook said as she was about to retreat. "I'll wait until you're-"

"No, bring it here," I instructed as I removed my gloves, "and tell All Furs to come up, please."

I knew the cook had to be wondering why I was being more hasty than usual, but I couldn't waste time. I needed to catch her in the act. As I waited, I dug my fingers into the soup and sure enough, I found a golden spindle at the bottom.

I was holding it up as Furs entered. She sounded out of breath, but still tried to greet me with a smile. "Is there something wrong?" she asked.

I was silent as my eyes stared at the bottom of Furs's coat. Beneath the pelts there was... leaves. "Do you have a dress on?" I asked.

Furs glanced down, and her eyes widened in alarm. "Oh, no. It's um..." She stammered and tried to conceal the fabric with her coat. However, as she moved, the glint of the gold ring caught my eye. I reached out and seized her hand.

I gently ran my fingers over the ring and looked to Furs. "I had placed this on Sam right before she left the ball." I smirked at her. "Care to explain why it is on your finger?"

Furs seemed to be at a loss for words. She then sighed, defeated, as she used her free hand to lower her hood to reveal the woodland's dress' tiara. Her face was covered in soot and dirt, but it was the same face I had been dancing with for the last three nights.

"Mysterious princess showing up and the appearance of golden treasures in my soup? It doesn't take much thought to see a connection between the two."

Sam sighed, sounding exhausted as she took a seat in a chair. "I figured you might guess, but I had hoped I could get away with a third night at least."

I pulled up a second chair and leaned forward. "Who are you exactly?"

She shut her eyes like she was recalling a bad dream. "I am - or was - Princess Samantha of Trolia."

I imagined Sam expected me to look shocked, but I wasn't. "I had thought so." I swallowed, unsure if I was allowed to ask this or not. "Is it true your father-"

"Wanted to marry me because I looked like my dead mother? Yes." She slumped in the chair and looked up at the ceiling. "The councillors had tried to persuade him to see reason, but he refused." She fingered the fur coat. "So, I told him that I would only marry him if he could find me a dress made from sunlight, a dress woven from the night sky, a dress sewn from the forest trees and a coat assembling the furs from every animal we had in the kingdom."

Troila was famous for it's trade in cloth making. It was said they made some of the finest silks in the word. It seemed like a challenge worthy enough to both stall and appease the king. That would also explain the theme of the trinkets left in the soup. They were

all related to sewing and cloth making. The spindle and wheel were obvious. And silk merchants knew that pulling a yard of silk through the ring was the best way to deduce if the silk was real or fake. Fake silk bunched against the metal while real silk glided through. These golden trinkets would be fitting for a princess of Troila.

Sam rubbed her tired eyes. "I had thought he would never be able to complete the gowns, or at least he would grow tired of me before he completed my request."

"But he didn't," I finished. "And he made the dresses and coat."

"Within three months, with the help of a zealous fairy godmother." Sam replied as she fiddled with her hair. "I realized I had to run away to escape him." She gave a bitter laugh. "The irony is that he had barely looked at me when I was a child, and the first time I got actual attention from him was when I didn't want it."

I reached out and squeezed her hand. "So, you've been living in the forest since you ran away? But King Louis has been dead for two years now," I asked. "Why do you still feel the need to hide? No one at my court would have cared."

Samantha gave a shrug as she wrapped her arms around herself. "Force of habit, I suppose? And even if my father is gone now, I can't go back to Trolia. There are too many bad memories there. And too many people who fear my return."

"All right," I replied as I fixed my skirt. "But, why did you come to the ball then?" I held up the golden trinkets. "And why put these in my soup?"

"The trinkets were my way of thanking you."

"Thanking me?" I asked surprised.

"There aren't many people that would give shelter to a wayward girl living in the woods," she bit her lower lip, "and you've become very precious to me." She gazed up at me with a sad smile. "Truth be told, Avery, you're the first person I felt I could trust since I left home. I dressed as a princess because ... I wanted to stay here but I also wanted to be able to talk to you on the same level."

I went quiet as my hands tightened into fists. "We were already talking on the same level. You were my friend as Furs. The first time I saw you as Sam... All I could think about was my friend in the kitchens."

Sam pouted "And then you forgot me until I dangled a mystery under your nose."

I laughed nervously "Well... to be fair, the mystery of the magical princess was equally fascinating."

We both giggled, sitting around the table, as the bread soup grew cold.

Samantha was clever, beautiful and kind. Sam was not someone to be pitied, she was someone to admire. Someone I should feel proud to call my Queen.

"Sam," I said as I took her hands gently. "Will you marry me?"

She looked up surprised. "You mean...you love me?"

"Of course I do," I said, and frowned. "You don't love me?"

"No, no, I do," she said, "but I didn't think you felt that way about me." She rubbed her neck and blushed. "That's why I wanted to keep my identity secret, so I wouldn't embarrass myself since I assumed you didn't."

"Well, I do, so I'll ask again," I repeated. "Will you marry me?"

I thought she would be hesitant, but she gently brushed my dark hair out of my eyes and kissed my cheek.

"Gladly."

I smiled as I engulfed her into a hug. We were married that spring, and both of my parents were overjoyed. Although, it did take a few tries to get my mother to fully understand that All Furs and Sam were one and the same. We made plans to spend our honeymoon in the woods so I could properly teach my Queen how to use a bow and an arrow. In return, she would teach me how to sew. Maybe at the next ball, I'll have a dress made of wind and clouds.

Nautilus
written by Ash Barnes
drawn by Elena "Yamino" Barbarich

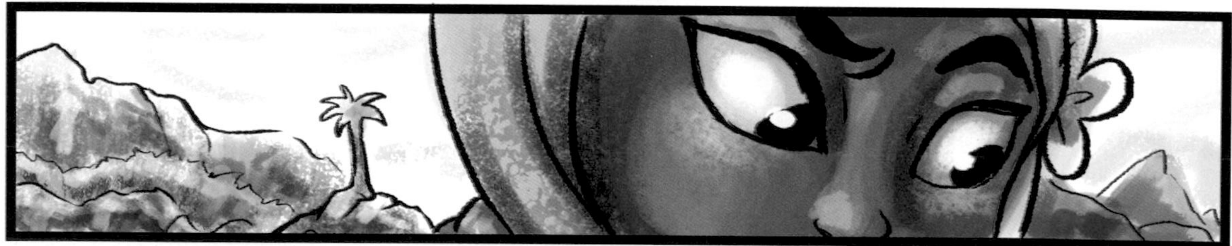

BREAK IT

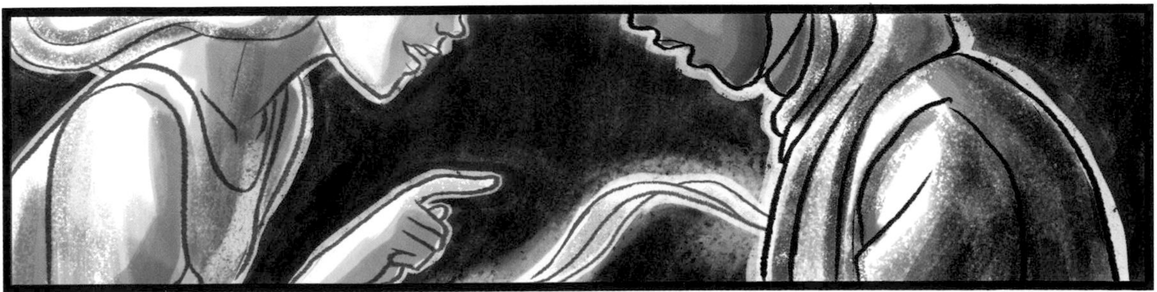

WHAT FEAR SAID
KATIE & STEVEN
SHANAHAN

huff
hah

huff
hah
huff
RATTLE
KLAK
KLAK

HATE TO SAY IT, BUT IF THE LEGENDS ARE TRUE, YOU KNOW WHAT'S IN THERE.

AND THAT IS WHY I MUST GO.
AND YET, HERE YOU STILL STAND.
FLAP FLAP
WHAT KEEPS YOU AT BAY? COULD IT POSSIBLY BE...

YOU'RE AFRAID?

FEH! I FEAR NOTHING.
OF COURSE...

...WE'RE JUST OUT HERE TO SEE WHAT A SHAKY SWORD FEELS LIKE.
KLAK
KLAK
RATTLE

LOOK, LET'S JUST BE REAL FOR A SECOND AND TALK THIS THROUGH.
LET'S JAM.
WHAT IS IT YOU ARE AFRAID OF?

I...

I...

THERE'S SOMETHING BAD IN THERE...
I CAN HEAR IT BREATHING... IT'S COMING TO GET ME.

I CAN'T WAKE UP. I'M SCARED!
M-MOMMY-HELP ME!

AH, AFRAID OF AN UNKNOWN BIG SCARY MONSTER, EH?
WELL, HOW ABOUT WE ASSUME THAT EVERYTHING WE HEARD IS TRUE.
IF WE EXPECT THE WORST, IT CAN'T TRULY BE ANY *WORSE* CAN IT?

OH, AND LET'S NOT FORGET,
YOU'RE THE ONE COMING TO 'GET' IT, SO...

nod

I'M AFRAID...

I'M AFRAID THAT IF IT JUMPS OUT AT ME FROM THE DARK...
CATCHING ME OFF GUARD,
I WON'T BE READY.

I COULD GET BADLY INJURED.
"RISE AND SHINE, CADET! THIS DAY IS GONNA HURT."
TRAINING. ACCIDENTS. BATTLES. "NO PAIN NO GAIN" SHOULD BE ALL TOO FAMILIAR.

BESIDES, YOU'VE SPENT YEARS WITH THAT SWORD.
FLIP
INSTINCT ALONE WILL HAVE IT UP IN FRONT BEFORE YOU EVEN KNOW YOU NEED IT.

A LITTLE JUMP SCARE WON'T BE YOUR END.

EVEN SO...

ALL MY TRAINING, MY ARMOR, IT MAY NOT BE ENOUGH.
IF ALL GOES WRONG, IT COULD VERY WELL KILL ME.

OOO, THAT'S POPULAR. IF IT'S DEATH YOU FEAR, YOU MAY HAVE TO GET IN LINE.
FUN FACT, THE WORLD'S SECOND GREATEST FEAR IS PUBLIC SPEAKING.

BUT IF I DIE, THOSE I LEAVE BEHIND, WHO DEPEND UPON ME, WILL SUFFER.

HMM, I AGREE YOU WILL BE MISSED DEARLY.
YET TIME WILL EASE THE STING AND THE WOUNDED WILL LIVE ON, CARRYING YOU IN THEIR MEMORIES. BUT I THINK YOU'VE TOUCHED ON SOMETHING...

IF I FAIL TO DESTROY IT...

IT MAY SOON COME FOR THE OTHERS.

IF IT LIVES ON...

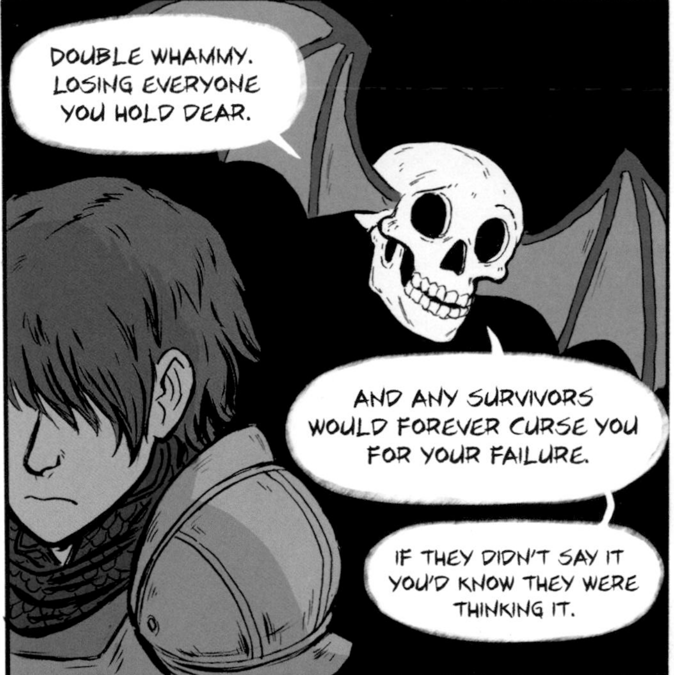
DOUBLE WHAMMY. LOSING EVERYONE YOU HOLD DEAR.
AND ANY SURVIVORS WOULD FOREVER CURSE YOU FOR YOUR FAILURE.
IF THEY DIDN'T SAY IT YOU'D KNOW THEY WERE THINKING IT.

OUR THOUGHT GAME IS NEARLY COMPLETE.
YOU DON'T ACTUALLY FEAR WHAT IS IN THIS CAVE, DO YOU NOW? YOU FEAR WHAT IT COULD MEAN...

WHAT I FEAR MOST...

...IS
BEING
ALONE.

AND THERE
WE ARE.
FOR EVERYTHING YOU'VE WORKED
TOWARDS, TO LEAD UP TO THAT END,
WELL, THAT WOULD BE A TRUE
TRAGEDY.

BUT AS WE'RE AWARE
OF WHAT'S AT STAKE,
WOULD IT NOT BE BEST
TO DO ALL WE CAN TO
PREVENT IT FROM
HAPPENING?
TAKE MATTERS
INTO YOUR OWN
HANDS!

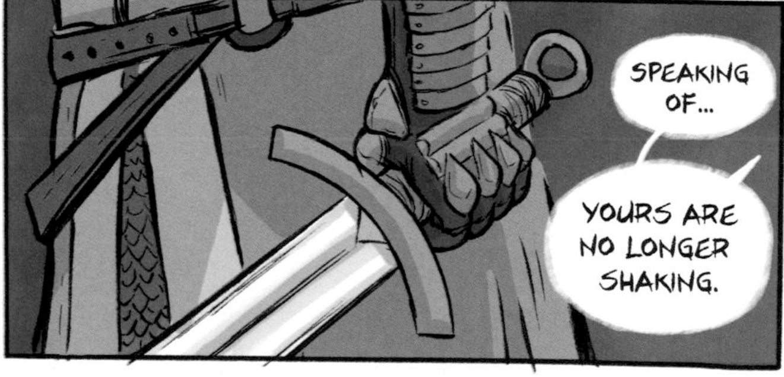
SPEAKING
OF...
YOURS ARE
NO LONGER
SHAKING.

HEH.
THANKS
FOR THAT.

SHKK

KLIK
KLAK
KLAK

HEH, JUST DON'T BE RECKLESS OR NOTHING.
AND IF YOU MAKE IT OUT ALIVE...

I'LL BE WAITING FOR YOU.

'TIL NEXT TIME.

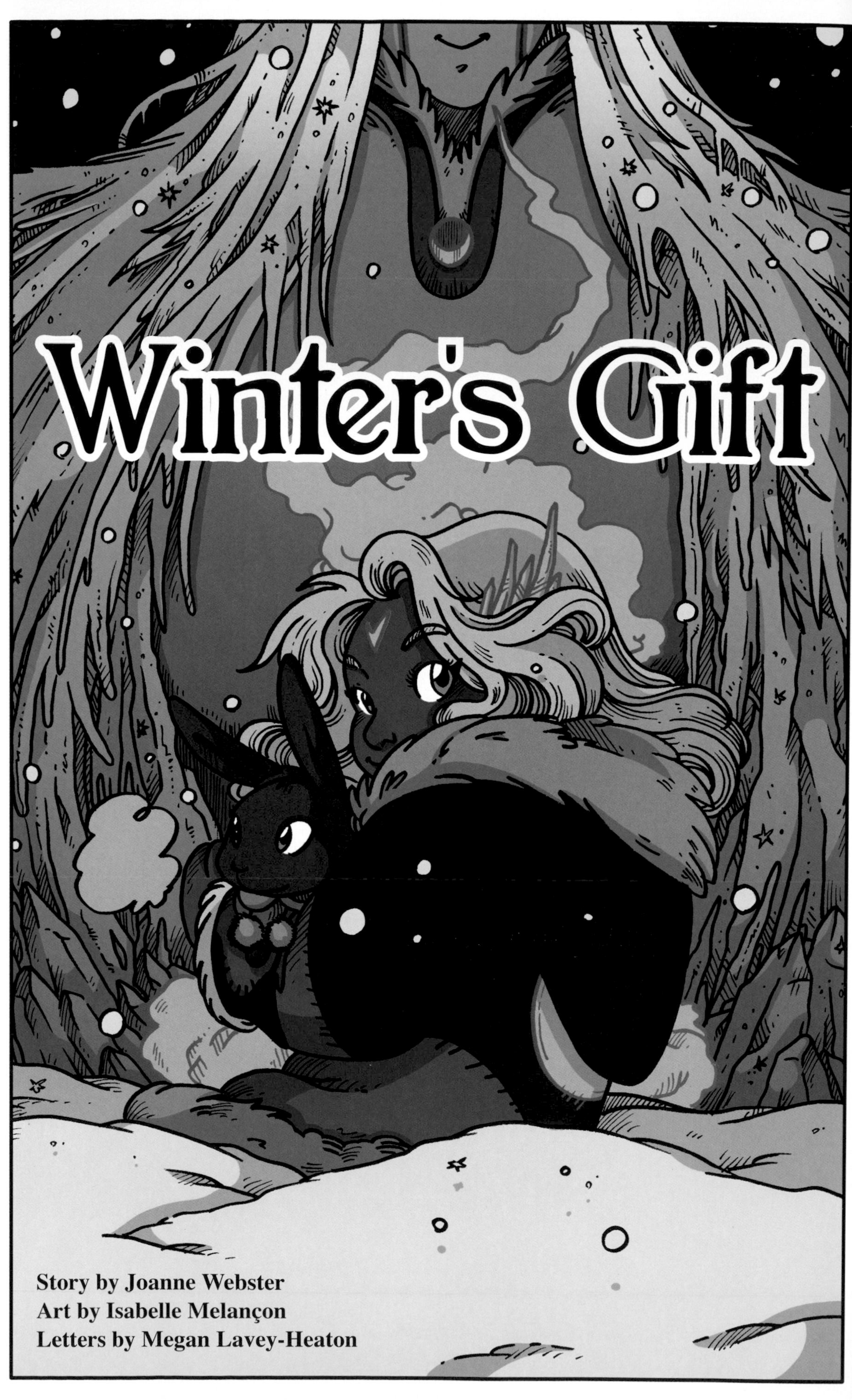

Winter's Gift
Story by Joanne Webster
Art by Isabelle Melançon
Letters by Megan Lavey-Heaton

LONG AGO, THE SEASONS OF SPRING, SUMMER, AND AUTUMN BESTOWED GIFTS ON THEIR FAVORITE ANIMALS.

SHARP TALONS WENT TO THE HAWKS. SPEED AND STRENGTH TO THE WOLVES. SWIFTNESS AND CUNNING TO THE FOXES.

TO THE RABBITS, THESE CHANGES IN THEIR PREDATORS BROUGHT FEAR.

IT'S NOT *FAIR!* WINTER WILL BE HERE SOON. WE'LL NEVER SURVIVE THE COLD AND THE SNOWS!

THERE'S A SOLUTION! WINTER HASN'T BESTOWED A GIFT YET! HE COULD HELP US!

WHY WOULD *HE* BOTHER? WINTER'S DARK AND COLD. HE DOESN'T CARE ABOUT US.

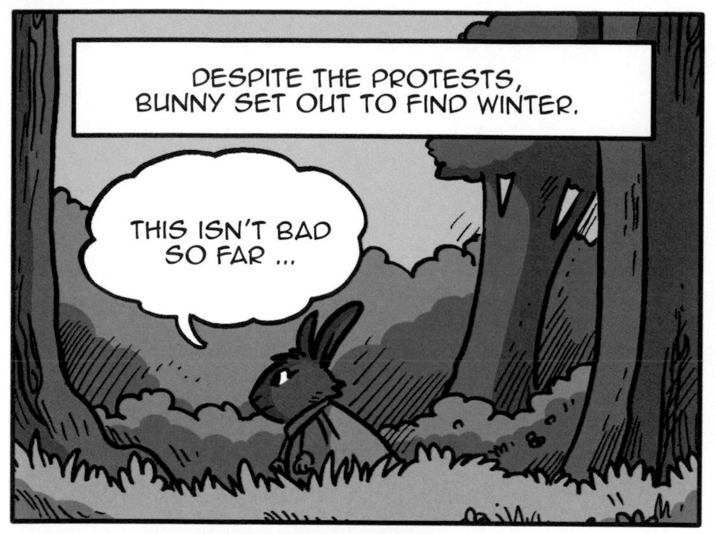

WHAT AN *ADORABLE* LITTLE RABBIT! WHY ARE YOU SO FAR FROM HOME?

I'M ON MY WAY TO SEE WINTER.

PLEASE, SPRING, LET ME PASS!

THERE! HOW'S YOUR NEW HOME? WE COULD ADD ***DAISIES*** TO THE BARS!

WELL, YES, THE CAGE IS VERY PRETTY ...

BUT SPRING, AREN'T YOU AFRAID OF SOMEONE BREAKING IN AND EATING ME?

FLOWERS AND VINES AREN'T THAT SOLID.

THIS IS THE FIRST TIME MY MEAL'S RUN TO ME.

I'M SORRY, SUMMER, BUT I'M **NOT** A MEAL.

I'M ON MY WAY TO SEE WINTER.

WINTER? **HE** HAS NO APPRECIATION FOR THE FINER DELICACIES SUCH AS YOURSELF.

DON'T WORRY. I'LL BE SURE TO APPRECIATE EVERY DELICIOUS BITE OF THE DINNER YOU'LL PROVIDE.

UM ... OK ... UH ... BUT HOW CAN YOU PROPERLY EAT ME IF YOU DON'T HAVE THE RIGHT SEASONINGS?
SEASONINGS?
HERBS THAT HELP MAKE A MEAL TASTIER. SURELY A FOOD EXPERT SUCH AS YOURSELF WOULD KNOW OF THEM.

OF *COURSE* I KNOW THEM.
YOU CAN'T COOK ME WITHOUT THEM.
THEN REMAIN HERE AND I'LL FETCH THEM.
THE RIGHT ONES ARE IN THE FAR SOUTH.

AS IF GOING TO THE FAR SOUTH WAS A CHALLENGE FOR SUMMER. I WILL BE BACK TO PREPARE YOU, MY DELICIOUS MEAL.

WHEW.

CRK!

WELL, WELL. A TINY RABBIT.

YOUR MAGNIFICENT FUR IS EXACTLY WHAT I NEED FOR A NEW HAT!

AGAIN?

... I'M SORRY. I CAN'T BECOME YOUR HAT. I MUST SEE WINTER!

HIM? HE HAS ***NO*** FASHION SENSE! HE WEARS NOTHING BUT WHITE. YOUR FUR WOULD BE SUCH A WASTE ON HIM.

STAY HERE WITH ME, AND YOU'LL HAVE THE GREAT HONOR OF BECOMING MY NEWEST HAT.
I SUPPOSE I'D MAKE A GOOD HAT. BUT WHAT WOULD YOU DECORATE ME WITH?

ARE YOU SUGGESTING I DON'T KNOW HOW TO DECORATE A HAT?
NO.

BUT ... UM ... SOMEONE LIKE *YOU* ...
SHOULD HAVE AN ***UNIQUE*** HAT DECORATED IN FEATHERS!

DON'T YOU THINK SO?

...
I *DO* LOOK AMAZING IN FEATHERS.

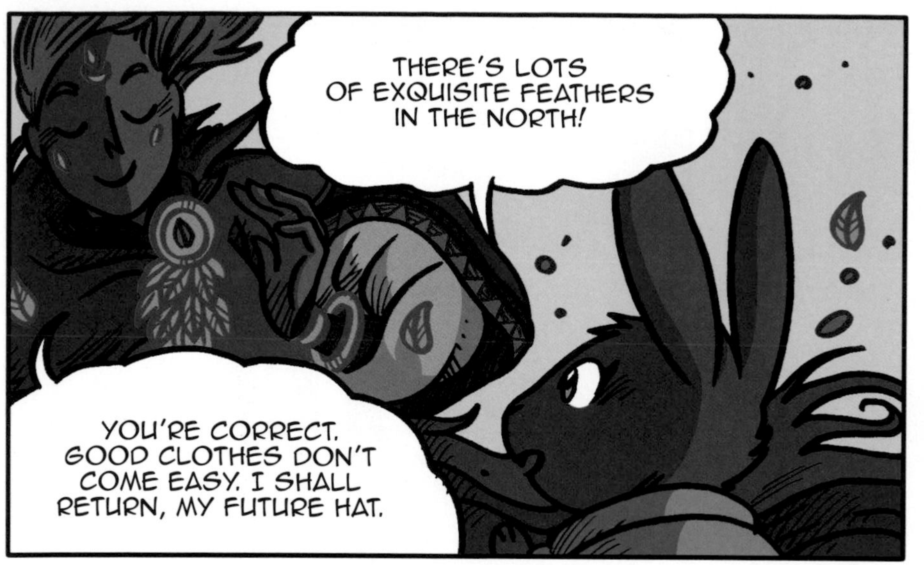
THERE'S LOTS OF EXQUISITE FEATHERS IN THE NORTH!
YOU'RE CORRECT. GOOD CLOTHES DON'T COME EASY. I SHALL RETURN, MY FUTURE HAT.

WHEW.

OH!

FFWOFF
HEE!!
WOOOO!!!

LITTLE RABBIT.
WHAT *ARE* YOU DOING?

WHY, I'M PLAYING IN THE SNOW!
THIS IS *NOT* A PLACE TO PLAY. DO YOU KNOW WHERE YOU ARE, OR WHO I AM?
YOU'RE WINTER!
I'VE COME A LONG WAY TO SEE YOU.

OH?
NO ONE BOTHERS TO COME SEE ME. WHY SHOULD YOU?

THE OTHER SEASONS HAVE BLESSED THE HUNTING ANIMALS. COULD YOU PLEASE GIVE THE RABBITS A BLESSING?

PERHAPS. BUT FIRST, HOW DID YOU REACH MY HOME?

THE ONLY WAY I COULD! I CROSSED THROUGH SPRING, SUMMER, AND AUTUMN.

THAT'S QUITE DANGEROUS. WEREN'T YOU AFRAID?

I'M NOT AFRAID OF THEM, NOR AM I AFRAID OF YOU.

WELL, YOU ***SHOULD*** BE AFRAID!

WINDS THAT HOWL. COLD THAT BITES.

THAT IS WINTER.

HOW'S THAT SCARY? I ***LOVE*** SNOW! I SNEAK OUT OF MY BURROW TO PLAY IN IT ALL THE TIME!

YOU'RE NOT JUST SAYING THAT TO PLEASE ME, ARE YOU?

WHY WOULD I? PLUS, YOU'RE NOT TRYING TO EAT ME OR TURN ME INTO CLOTHES LIKE THE OTHER SEASONS.

YOU ARE THE FIRST TO TRAVEL THIS FAR AND TO SPEAK KINDLY TO ME.

ALLOW ME TO USE MY WINDS TO ESCORT YOU HOME.

DEAR RABBITS!
I HAVE COME TO PRESENT YOU WITH A GIFT!
DURING WINTER, YOUR FUR WILL TURN AS WHITE AS SNOW SO THAT YOU MAY HIDE FROM THE HUNTERS WHO STALK YOU.

NOT ONLY WILL YOUR FUR TURN WHITE IN THE WINTER, BUT I HAVE ENCHANTED YOUR COAT SO YOU SHALL GAIN A HUMAN FORM LIKE I HAVE.

POOF!

OH, THANK YOU!

THANK YOU SO MUCH, WINTER!

YES.

FROM THEN ON, BUNNY WOULD SPEND HER SPRING AND SUMMERS WITH HER FAMILY. COME AUTUMN SHE WOULD DON HER COAT AND SPEND THE REMAINDER OF THE YEAR WITH HER HUSBAND.

THEY SAY WHENEVER YOU SEE SNOWFLAKES AS LARGE AND FLUFFY AS A RABBIT'S TAIL, IT'S BECAUSE WINTER IS HAPPILY THINKING ABOUT HIS WIFE.

AND THEIR LOVE WAS ETERNAL, JUST LIKE THE SEASONS.

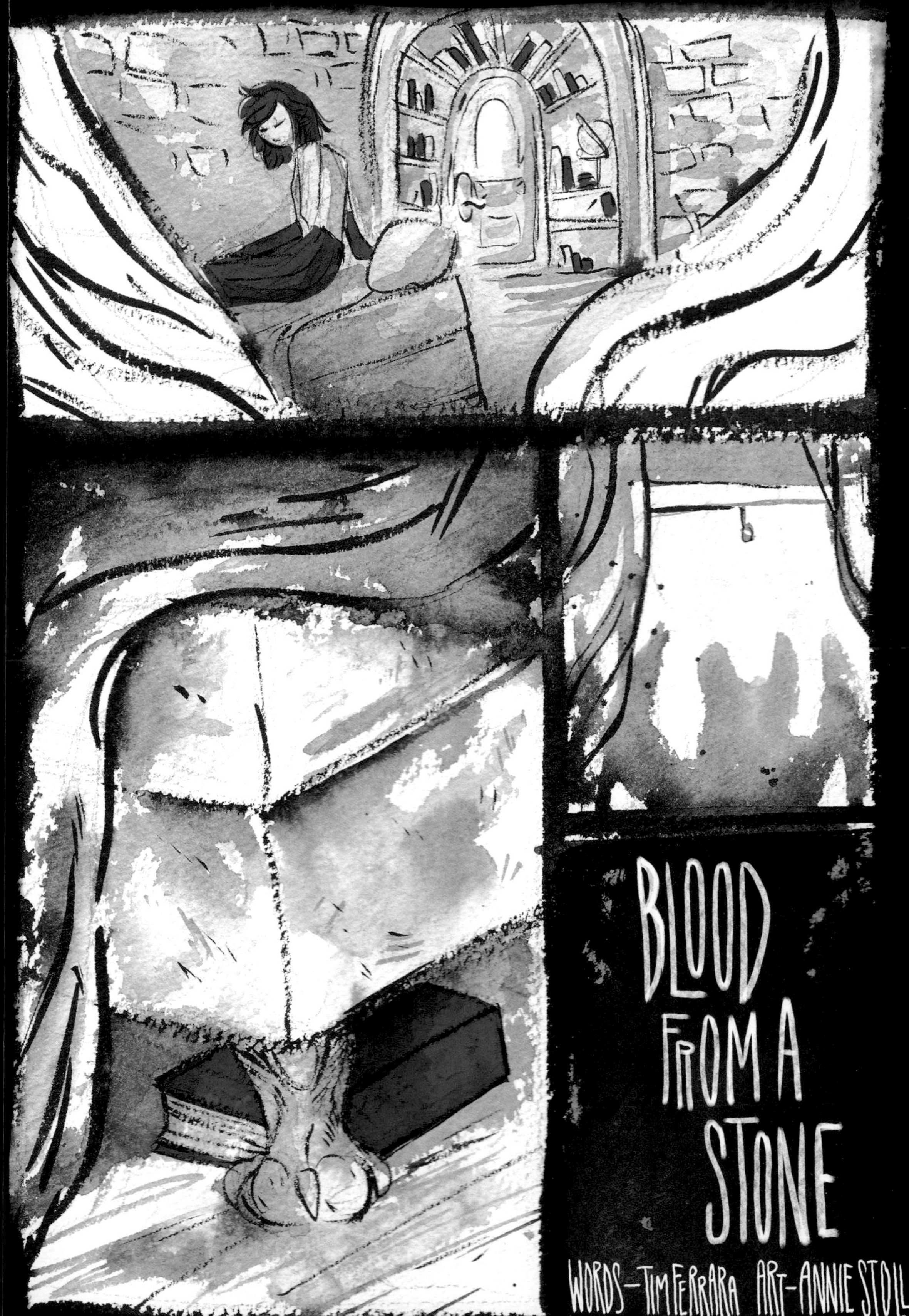
BLOOD FROM A STONE
WORDS—TIM FERRARA ART—ANNIE STOLL

YOU'RE NOT FRIGTHENED ?

Should I be?

WELL... IT'S A LITTLE STRANGE, A STATUE KNOCKING

ON A PERSON'S WINDOW.

Oh, I suppose it is. Gargoyles watch over the Cities. They protect us.

I DON'T THINK I COULD PROTECT MUCH OF ANYTHING, TO BE HONEST. I'M DREADFULLY SMALL...THAT'S WHY I'VE COME HERE. YOU HAVE MAGIC—

Magic isn't allowed. I could get in trouble.

THIS HASN'T STOPPED YOU.

Well... no.

What is it you wanted? I could try to make you bigger.

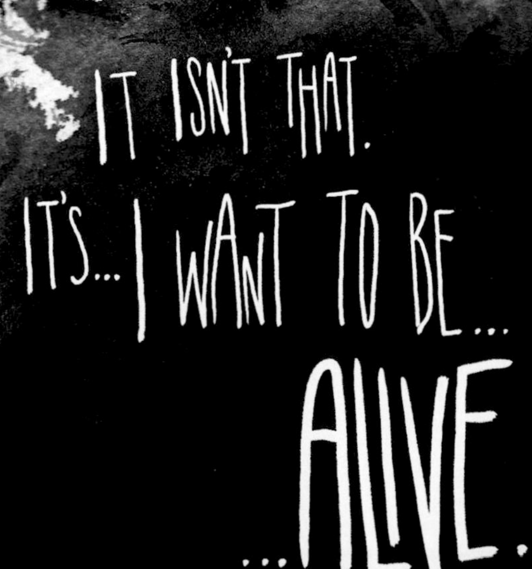

IT ISN'T THAT.
IT'S... I WANT TO BE...
...ALIVE.

Alive?
MADE FLESH....
FREED FROM THIS STONE BODY.
Then...
I'll try my best!

WELL??!!
The first step is to find out how alive you need to be.
Do you have a soul?

DOES HAVING A SOUL MAKE ONE ALIVE?

Having a soul makes you *you*.

I DON'T KNOW IF I HAVE ONE.

Why don't we just focus on your physical body right now.

Let's start with growth. Bodies need to grow, right?

IF YOU SAY SO.

Hm.
Let's try breath. Living body's got to breathe!

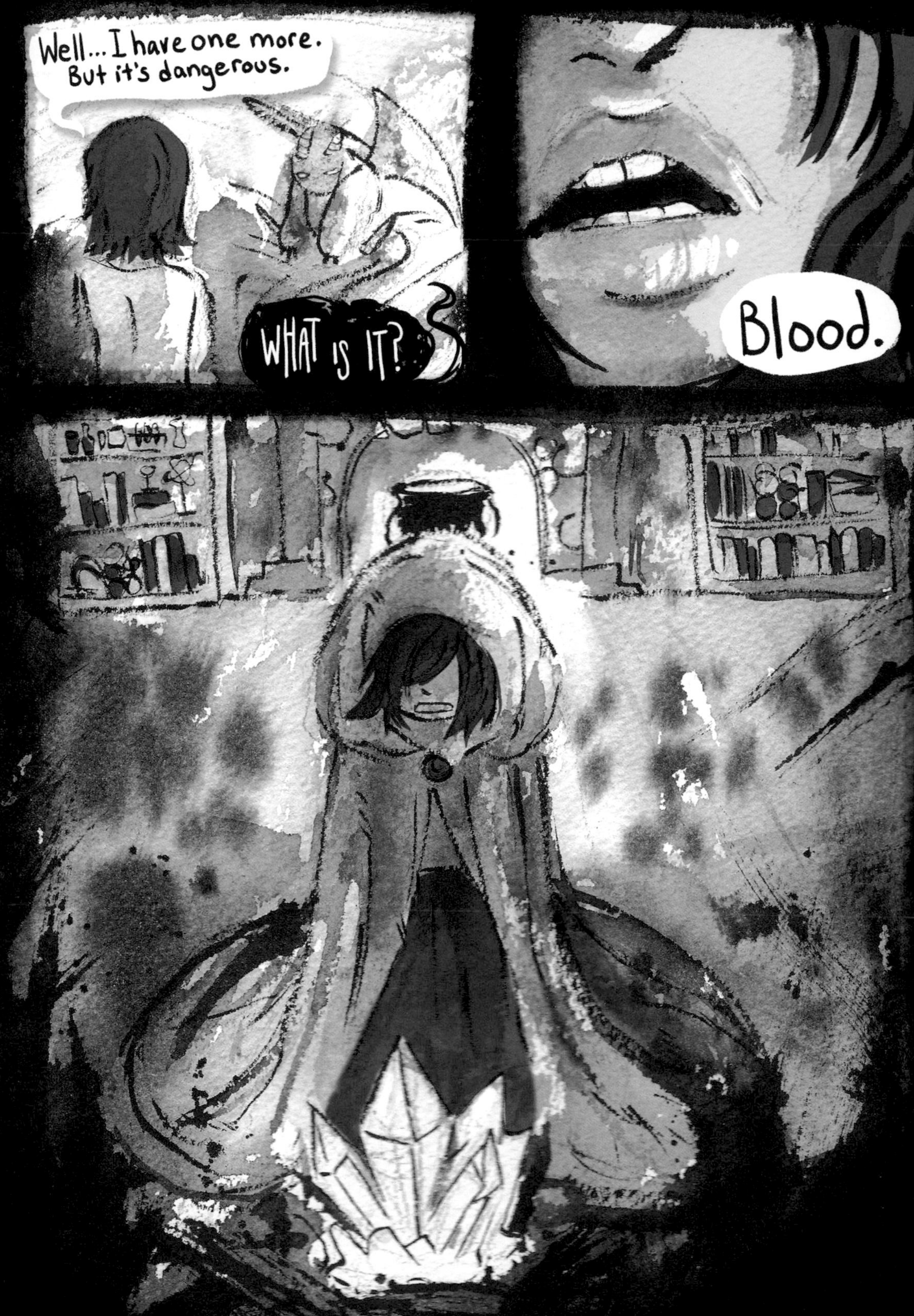
Well... I have one more.
But it's dangerous.
WHAT IS IT?
Blood.

IS IT SUPPOSED TO DO THAT?
Something's wrong!

AT LONG LAST I AM FREE!!

AND SO....

HUNGRY!!

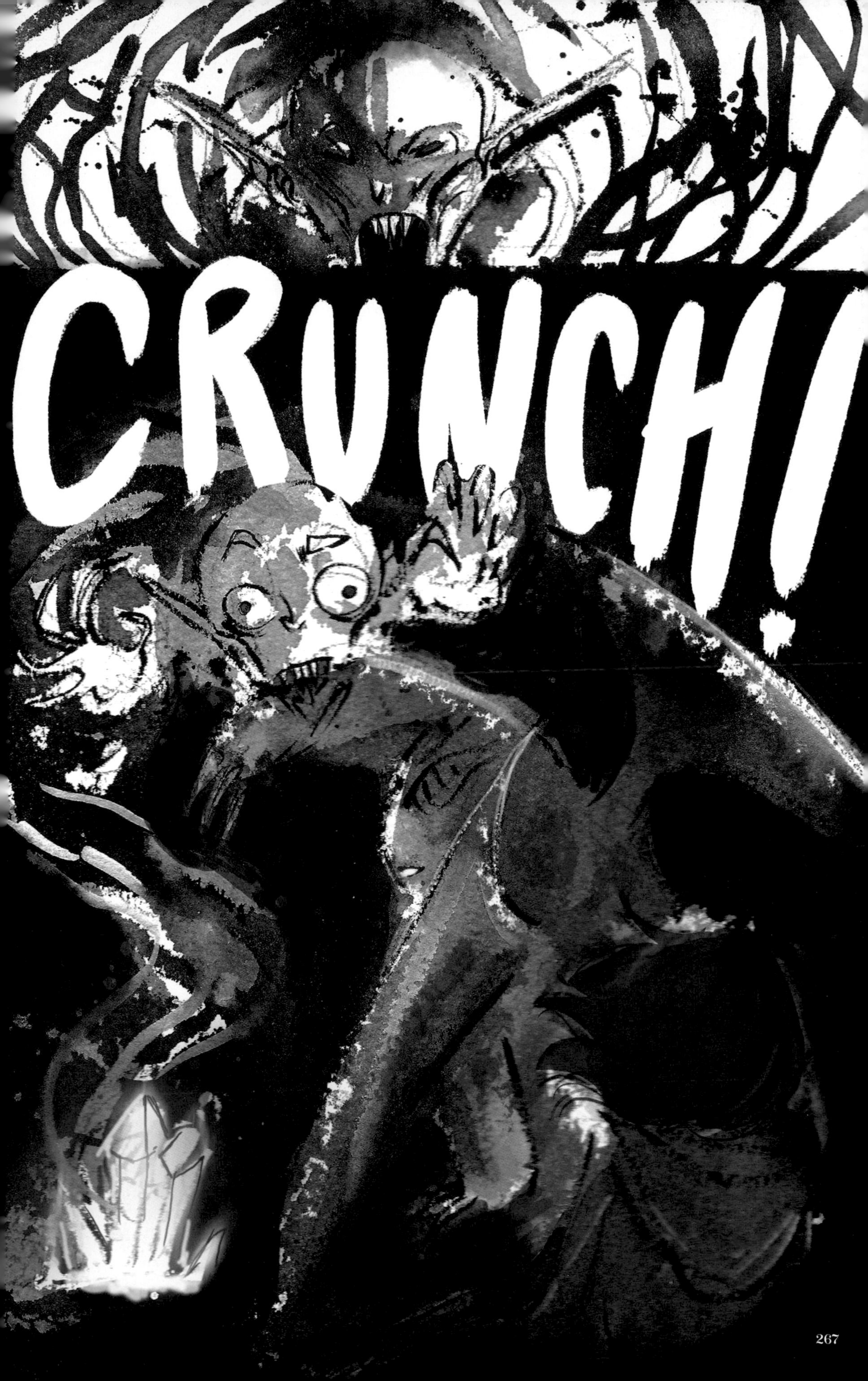
CRUNCH!

YOU WON'T HURT HER!

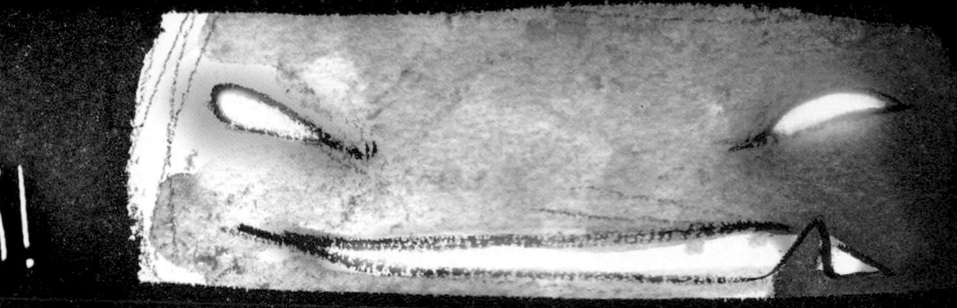

RWAAAH!!!

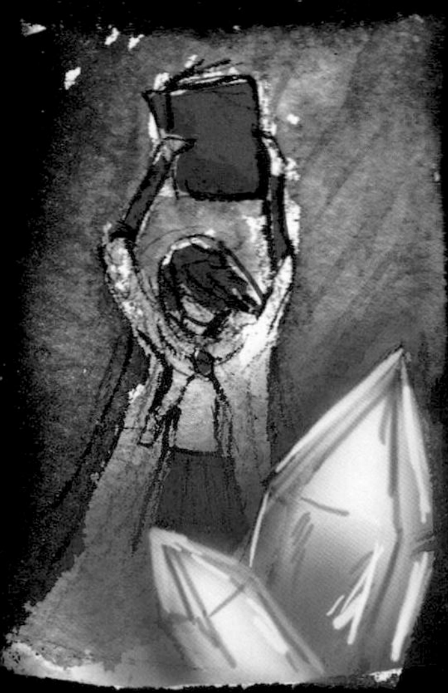

I'm so sorry! I can try again.
NO NEED. YOU WERE RIGHT TO QUESTION ME EARLIER. FOR THE FIRST TIME, I FEEL
I'M SUPPOSED TO BE.
Well... for what it's worth
I'm really glad that you're you.

Story by Megan Lavey-Heaton | Art by August Brown

In a time that was once and put upon, there lived a girl named Finette. They said that she was the youngest daughter of a king and queen who could no longer afford to feed their three daughters. They had turned their attention to making nets, a more profitable venture than running a kingdom.

The eldest daughter was promptly married off. The middle daughter fled and became a nun. Or a pirate. The gossips weren't quite sure which one was correct.

But then there was the youngest, who was sent to become the apprentice to the matron of an orphanage who happened to be an Ogress. The matron stripped her of her true name, and she was dubbed Finette.

And in that orphanage there also lived twelve other girls and three little boys, also named Finette.

"Really? *Really?*" Finette groaned as the matron accepted yet another slightly confused and crying foundling and declared them the latest Finette. "Could you not think of any other name for the group of us? Mary or George or even Patrick is really quite nice. But Finette? 16 of us?"

"18," the matron pronounced and dumped two squirming bundles in Finette's arms. "These are twins!"

"Terrific." Finette stared into the identical faces of two little boys, destined to carry on the cobbled-together tradition of atrocious names. "Well, come on then Seventeen and Eighteen," she said, rattling off their order in the Finette line rather than their new names. "You need your nappies changed."

With a wheeze and a groan, the matron took herself off to tally up the latest in government assistance funds she would be able to collect with the appearance of the newest Finettes. The first Finette changed the babies, scrubbed the floor, cooked dinner, mended stockings, and did everything that the Ogress was paid to do but usually foisted off on her.

"I used to be a princess," Finette muttered to one of the babies, who sucked his fist and stared at the ceiling. "I had pretty dresses and servants and books. So, so many books. But, no, my mother and dad wanted to make nets instead. I wonder if I should go off to make my fortune. I do believe I'm quite old enough. I'm 19, or at least I think I am. I can do anything I set my mind to. Isn't that right, Seventeen?" She quickly double-checked the note she pinned to the baby's nappy to tell him and his twin apart. "Yes. Seventeen."

It took Finette a few days to decide upon what fortune she wanted to seek. Money was nice. Fame didn't hold a lot of interest for her. Marriage wasn't something she wanted at all. She'd taken care of enough babies in her life, thank you very much, and didn't want any of her own. She had training to be a nursemaid or a serving girl, but surely there was something else she could aspire to since she was once a princess. Fortune hunting could not be undertaken at a moment's notice, she told Seventeen.

"I believe," she decided after a long day when it was nearly impossible to tell the other 17 Finettes apart, "I shall go in search of proper names for you all. You must have had them at one point."

So the day that the Ogress crafted new birth certificates for the twins, Finette convinced the second-oldest Finette to impersonate her. She kissed all the other children on their foreheads and told them she was off in search of a fairy godmother. She also took Seventeen with her.

"You know too much," she informed the little boy, contently asleep as she nestled him into a sling that would hold him close to her chest. "Why, they could make you talk. I know you're a few months old, but I think Finette XIII knows just enough magic to be dangerous and I'm not taking any chances. I'll get you back to your brother soon, and you will have proper names."

On her way out, Finette stole the birth certificates the Ogress had created and the amount of coins that made up Seventeen's share of government assistance. And off she went to find her fairy godmother.

"I must have one somewhere," she told Seventeen that first night, as they camped out beside the road and the baby fussed for hours because he was teething. "I think it's a princess rule. There's a fairy godmother or a benefactor or a prince out there. I'm not that interested in princes. Or princesses. That means I have to rule a kingdom, and look how that turned out for my parents. No, I think I'll travel. Maybe I'll learn magic. I also make an incredible awesome pie. How about a traveling chef? You can be my apprentice, once you're old enough to hold a bowl and not fall into it."

Fortune hunting, Finette learned, was a very tedious chore. Especially when you were toting a baby with you. But babies got you into places where poor, bedraggled girls usually couldn't go. Like squeezed into the last bit of space on a traveling coach. Or a bed of clean, soft rags in the corner of an inn's kitchen. People took pity on an infant and accepted the woman attached to it. This was something Finette was used to. No one paid attention to the person caring for the baby, rather the baby himself. And Seventeen was good-natured and didn't fuss much.

In the fifth town, Finette discovered the circuit judge would arrive within two days. She decided she didn't need a fairy godmother, rather she needed a court order. Court orders were pretty powerful, she informed Seventeen as she swept the kitchen of the inn where they stayed. She cleaned and baked in exchange for a tiny room under the stairs, and when she could, she consulted a baby name book she borrowed from a nearby church. She constructed a list of 17 perfectly respectable names and attached them to the false birth certificates the Ogress provided. On the second day, she bundled up Seventeen and went to visit the judge.

She sat through a murder trial, three custody hearings, and the public mocking of a mime. As the sun started to set, the judge finally agreed to hear her case. Straightening her frayed skirts, Finette approached the bench and told her story to the judge.

"And here is the list of names I created," she said, putting the stack of documents in front of her.

The judge frowned at the documents. "Is this some sort of joke?"

"I assure you, your honor, it is no joke."

"You told me you didn't want their names to be Finette."

"That is correct."

"Then why is Finette written 17 times?"

Finette snatched the certificates out of the judge's hands and gasped. Where there had been line after line of neatly written and perfectly respectable names the night before, all of them were replaced with the word "Finette" in her handwriting.

As Finette sputtered and the baby fussed, the judge ordered her from the courtroom. This involved being escorted out by two burly guards, because Finette was far too busy being shocked and begging the judge to hear her out to bother paying attention to the rules. When she and Seventeen found themselves left on the roadside, she grumbled and shoved the documents back in her satchel.

"We'll find another judge," she told Seventeen, "and try again."

So Finette and Seventeen traveled to the next town and appealed to the judge there. Then to the mayor in another town and a priest in a third. Night after night, Finette wrote down 17 names for 17 orphans. Day after day, the names were replaced with Finette.

"Finette, Finette, Finette times infinity!" she cried as they were turned away again, perilously close to tears. She had gone through most of the funds she'd stolen from the Ogress, and word about the odd name-seeking girl and the baby she carried had spread about enough that finding work was impossible. "I am so sick of that name! I wish I'd never heard of it."

In anger, she whirled around and hurled the birth certificates into a water trough. Instead of melting into a messy, inky blob, they floated on the surface of the dirty water. Finette stared at them, a little dumbfounded. Carefully, she approached the trough and lifted a single certificate. She gave it a sharp shake, and the water rolled off it, leaving the certificate as dry and pristine as the day it was created.

"This is magic," Finette cried and set out to prove it. She dumped an entire bottle of ink on the pile of certificates. She shoved them in a fire and left them in the road to be crushed by passing carriages. Every time, the certificates emerged looking like new.

So in the next town, Finette went to the local magic guild and made her case.

"These are indeed magic," the guild leader informed her. "They are tied to the magical signature of each child. Ogress magic is very powerful indeed, and it is causing all of your attempts to change the children's names to fail."

"But why would the Ogress do that?" Finette asked.

"That I do not know. But I don't have the power to change these names. If you find out, you could break the magic."

So Finette and Seventeen started the long journey back to the orphanage. Long journeys are excellent for thinking, and Finette spent the days mulling over theories and working out reasons why the Ogress would give them all the same name. The day they reached their kingdom, instead of going to the orphanage, Finette found herself wandering to the tavern just down the road. She sat on a bench out front and wondered if it was even worth a try.

The door burst open, and the circuit judge that turned Finette away to begin with strode out. The judge halted the cluster of lawyers and clerks that followed her and turned to the girl. "It is you again, the girl of the made-up names."

Finette scrambled off her bench, causing Seventeen to fuss. "They're magic! The certificates are magic. It's causing the list to change, I swear it. I had a magic guild prove it and everything. Why would an ogress want eighteen children named Finette?"

"Seventeen false Finettes," the judge said, "and one true one."

Finette blinked. "Me?"

"No." The judge indicated the baby in Finette's arm. "The boy."

"Seventeen?" Finette stared into the baby's face as he settled down. "He's a true Finette?"

"Hand me the certificates."

Finette handed them over, and the judge sorted through them, muttering an incantation under her breath. The certificates lifted into the air and began to glow. All turned red except one, which changed to a bright green and floated into the tiny hands of the baby that Finette held.

"My sister," the judge told Finette, "runs the magic guild you visited. She informed me of your case, and I agreed to take another look at it. There have been reports of children being abducted after a prophecy was made that a young prince or princess known as Finette would grant them immense power and weath. Your Ogress was in search of that true Finette. He is the heir to a vast kingdom in the north and was stolen from his cradle, along with his twin. But Ogres are not very intelligent and started stealing every baby they could get their hands on and hoped to get lucky. That's why you were all named Finette. If the name was true, she would be able to tell with the birth certificates. Then she would eat the true Finette and absorb his magical signature, thus becoming the heir herself."

Finette frowned and held the baby closer to her chest. "Then why didn't she eat the rest of us?"

"You're worth far more to her in government assistance than you ever were as food."

"So how can we all get proper names?"

"You must break the Ogress' magic. Once it's broken, the certificates will be invalid, and I can give you all new names."

Finette returned to the orphanage with Seventeen and placed him in the cradle with Eighteen. They'd been gone for five weeks, but Finette II did such an excellent job as an impersonator that the Ogress never noticed. She resumed her life of cleaning and baking and changing nappies. Whenever she could, she sneaked to the library to research magic. What she found was a bit distasteful, but she had to do it. So Finette returned to the orphanage and started to bake. She baked and baked and baked until she used all of the government assistance money. And still she baked until the matron finally took notice and came down to the kitchen.

"You wasteful girl," she yelled at Finette. "You have spent all our money for the month and the next three months after. How am I going to afford my bingo games?"

"But they're your favorite," Finette said sweetly.

The matron took a muffin and ate it. Then she ate another and another. She ate so many that after awhile, she curled up beneath the table and fell into a deep sleep. As she slept, Finette brought the certificates to her and knelt by her side. She told the sleeping Ogress matron of her long journey, of discovering Seventeen's true heritage. She talked about the cookbook she found on how to eat babies and absorb their magical signatures. She also talked at length about the research she conducted on Ogre magic.

"I really have no desire to kill anyone, for I am not an Ogress," she informed the snoozing matron. "And I'm really not one for confrontation either. But as long as you affix your fingerprint to each of these letters I have drafted allowing the magic to be broken, all of us will be allowed to have true names."

So she took the Ogress' hand and inked the fingertips well. She pressed a finger to each of the seventeen letters she drafted, freeing each child from their loathed name. As she did, the birth certificate for each child shimmered and began to change. They became fragile paper once more, revealing the true name of each child. There were a couple of Marys, three Pattys, and a Julianna. The very last certificate to change was Finette's own. She sat on her heels and beheld the real name that her parents had given her. Then she quickly ushered the other children out of the house and left the sleeping matron behind for the authorities to arrest.

The judge was waiting for Finette, along with duly appointed guardians to help find the other children homes. "You are an adult," she told Finette, "and can make your own way in the world. What will you do with your life?"

"I'm not sure," Finette replied. "But I do want to get the real Finette and his brother back to his parents. Then maybe I'll be a chef or a writer or a card shark. I can be anything I want."

"I see. And what was your true name, girl?"

A smile tugged at the corner of Finette's lips. "Why, that's a secret. I'll tell the right person one day. But if I tell you now, then you will tell me I have to go rule a kingdom or marry a prince, and I really have no desire to do that."

The judge shook her head. "Well, off you go then, in search for your happily ever after."

"Happily ever afters are for princesses," Finette declared and started down the road with the twin boys. "I'd rather be happy."

BY KADI FEDORUK

THE DOCTOR WILL COME AGAIN TONIGHT.
SEND VASILISA IN.

DON'T TIRE HER OUT TOO MUCH.

YOU'VE GROWN INTO SUCH A BEAUTIFUL YOUNG WOMAN, MY DARLING.

I HAVE A GIFT FOR YOU, I'VE KEPT IT CLOSE TO MY HEART.

GIVE HER A LITTLE TO EAT WHEN YOU ARE TROUBLED. SHE WILL HELP YOU IN MY STEAD.

MOTHER SAID TO FEED YOU WHEN I WAS FEELING TROUBLED. NOTHING COULD BE WORSE THAN THIS.

DO NOT BE SAD, VASILISA. IT WILL LOOK BRIGHTER TOMORROW.

DO NOT BE AFRAID. YOUR FATHER WILL RETURN BEFORE YOU KNOW IT.

I BROUGHT YOU BACK A NEW MOTHER, VASILISA. TWO SISTERS, TOO. A GROWING GIRL NEEDS A MOTHER.

I DON'T THINK THEY LIKE ME.
I WILL PROTECT YOU. SLEEP. IT WILL LOOK BRIGHTER TOMORROW.

CLANG
CLANG

YOU'RE LATE. MAKE US BREAKFAST.

PETYR CAME THIS MORNING TO ASK FOR VASILISA.
AGAIN?

SHE HAS **NO** SENSE OF PROPRIETY.
I LIKED HIM. I CAN'T BELIEVE HER.
WHY DO THEY ALL WANT HER?

DARLINGS, GO PICK SOME FLOWERS FOR YOUNG PETYR.

SHOW HIM HE CHOSE THE WRONG MAIDEN.

GAH!
WOULD YOU LIKE SOME HEL--

SORRY ABOUT THAT, I'M MORE HINDRANCE THAN HELP, IT SEEMS.

I'D BE DELIGHTED TO FIX MY MISTAKE.

GIRLS, IT'S TIME FOR THAT PLAN WE DISCUSSED.

I HAVE TWO DAUGHTERS TO MARRY OFF BEFORE HER. TRUE LADIES. NOT SOME TRASH.
MADAME, I'M--
I COULDN'T CARE LESS WHO YOU ARE.
THANK YOU FOR THE HELP.
SHUSH, YOU.
WHY IS IT SO DARK?
OH VASILISA, ALL THE FIRES ARE OUT. WHATEVER WILL WE DO?
GO TO BABA YAGA AND BRING BACK A LIGHT.
AND DON'T COME BACK UNLESS YOU HAVE IT.
THEY'RE JUST SENDING ME TO BE EATEN BY BABA YAGA.
DO NOT BE AFRAID VASILISA. I WILL PROTECT YOU.

WHAT, OR WHO, WAS THAT?
I DON'T HAVE ANY FOOD FOR YOU...OR ME.
I HOPE WE'RE GOING THE RIGHT WAY.
RIDER, HOW DO I GET TO BABA YAGA?

MUST BE GETTING CLOSE NOW.

I CAN SMELL YOU, CHILD. HERE FOR MY SUPPER?

I NEED TO BRING LIGHT BACK TO MY FAMILY.

I KNOW THAT FAMILY WELL.

I WILL GIVE YOU LIGHT, BUT YOU MUST SORT MY GRAIN, CLEAN THE POPPY SEEDS AND COOK MY MEAL BEFORE I RETURN ON THE MORROW. OR I WILL GRIND YOUR BONES FOR MY BREAD.

OH. OH DEAR.

DO NOT DESPAIR, VASILISA. OPEN ME AND DISCARD MY SHELL. I WILL PROTECT YOU WITH YOUR MOTHER'S BLESSING.

COOK HER DINNER, VASILISA. I WILL CLEAN THE POPPY.

THANK YOU FOR ALL YOUR HARD WORK. I COULDN'T DO THIS WITHOUT YOU.

BABA YAGA RETURNS. THROW MY FINAL HUSK IN THE FIRE AND RETRIEVE THE LIGHT. DO NOT ASK HER ANYTHING ABOUT THIS HOUSE.

SHAME I WON'T HAVE FRESH MEAT TONIGHT.

BANG
BANG

TAKE THE WHEAT AND GRIND IT.

DO YOU HAVE ANY QUESTIONS, CHILD?

ПШЕНИЦА

...YES.

WHO WERE THOSE RIDERS I PASSED?

HMM, THE RIDERS?

THE WHITE RIDER, MY DAY. THE RED RIDER, MY SUN. THE BLACK RIDER, MY NIGHT.

ANYTHING ELSE?
VASILISA, NO. DON'T ASK *HER* ANYTHING ELSE, JUST GO HOME WITH YOUR BOON.
WELL...
NO?
THEN I HAVE A QUESTION. HOW DID YOU COMPLETE MY IMPOSSIBLE TASKS?
BY... MY MOTHER'S GIFT AND BLESSING.
I DON'T NEED A BLESSED CHILD. MORE TROUBLE THAN THEY'RE WORTH.
TAKE THE LIGHT YOU'VE EARNED AND LEAVE.

ALMOST...ALMOST BACK TO THAT HOUSE.

WAIT.

LET ME RETURN THE LIGHT.

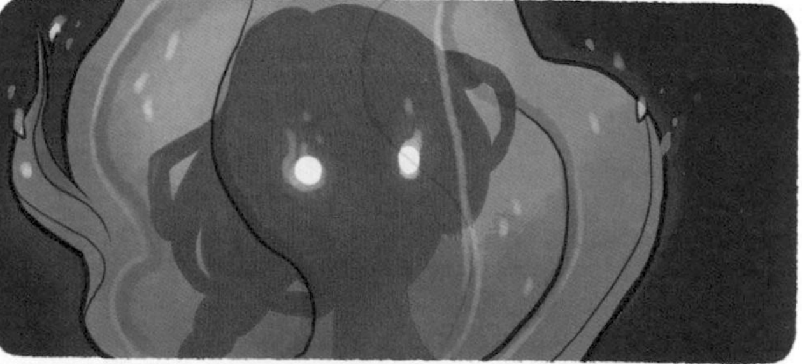

LIVE FOR YOURSELF, MY DARLING.

BATOOOM

MOTHER!

HOT!

NO
NO
NO NONO
NONONONO.

PLEASE.
NO
SNIFFFF

BABA YAGA'S LIGHT WAS A CURSE. I COULD NOT LET YOU BE THE ONE TO DESTROY THEM.
FORGET ABOUT ALL THIS HORROR. GO TO THE CITY, LEARN A TRADE, FIND LOVE. NOTHING STANDS IN YOUR WAY.
BUT IT'S SO HORRIBLE.

GOODBYE.

WITH THE EVIL FAMILY DEAD, VASILISA TRAVELLED TO THE BIG CITY, AND CAUGHT THE EYE OF A YOUNG MAN. BUT THAT IS ANOTHER STORY.

THANK YOU

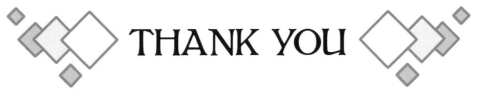

Valor would not be possible without our family, friends, and the support from the following people who backed our Kickstarter in 2014.

"Action Science" Dinerman Family
3Jane
a k sarah
A loyal fan
A. Camner
A. Gregory
A. K. Proctor
A. Léguillon
A. M. Carr
A. Miura
A.Buck
A.D.
A.J. Dal Santo
Aaron & Charlotte Churchill
Aaron Alberg
Aaron M. Wilson
Abbie Gore
Abby Wilson
Abby! Witherell
Abigail Rice
Abrian Curington
Achi Sea Cucumber
Acillus (Lee B.)
Ada Puigarnau
Adam Beardsley
Adam Bell
Adam Sjoberg
Adam Van Wyk
Adam Wesley Sturm
Adam Whitcomb
Addy F
Adrian A. Gallegos
Adriane Ruzak
Adrien Boulanger
Adrienne Ankuda
Adrienne Galasso
Aestrix
AG Prigent
Ahmad Moghrabi
Aiden Bingman
Ailsa L
AJ Carruthers
AJ Hagan
AJ917
Alaina Mossman
Alan & Amanda
Alan Morgan
Alana Christie
Alana Joli Abbott
Alanna Jones
Albireo
Ale M.
Alec Hauser
Alen Syhn
Alex
Alex Chaikin
Alex Fux
Alex Grandstaff
Alex Hammond
Alex L
Alex Ledum
Alex Lupp
Alex M.
Alex Neumeister
Alex Price
Alex Putnam
Alex Stepanek
Alexa Van Vliet
Alexander
Alexander Speaks
Alexandra Brown
Alexandra Burkot
Alexandra Mayer
Alexandra Vasquez
Alexandra Wimberley
Alexandria Gray
Alexikakon
Alexis & Richard Robinson
Alexis Fresquez
Alexis Jubilee Ruiz
Alexis McAdams
Alice A
Alice Bennett
Alice Bentley
Alice Bourdykina-Jelobniouk
Alice Felberg
Alice Mae Cook
Alice Takagawa
Alice Toshi
Alicia N. Mitchell
Alicia S Avril
Alicia Sartori
Alina Casales
Aline Juliette
Alisa Bishop
Alisha Claypool
Alisha VanHoose Torres
Alison 'Purplefire' Dubbert
Alison Bacon
Alison Benowitz
Alison Graham
Alison R
Alison Scribailo
Alissa R.
Alix Evans
Alix Z.
Alix/Lithaenia
Allie Peusch
Allison Chipman
Allison Daugherty
Allison Liu
Allison Usher
Ally Kaiser
Allyn C. Iwane
Allyssa Sleezer
Almudena Bernardos
Alok Baikadi
Alopeks
Alyce Evans
Alycia Joy Shedd
Alys Tanner
Alysa Miller
Alyss Barnes
Alyssa
Alyssa Cedoz
Alyssa Fox
Alyssa Summers
Alyxe Barron
Amalie Steidley
Amanda Ahlstrom
Amanda Bernetsky
Amanda Bizune
Amanda Cluff
Amanda Cosmos
Amanda Dier
Amanda Helman
Amanda Munson
Amanda P.
Amanda R Borrelli
Amanda Scott
Amanda Vidales
Amanda Webb, mandapanda rawks
Amber Choquette
Amber D.
Amber J Cartier-Page
Amber Lanagan
Amber McBratney
Amber Siomara
Amber Skye Engelmann
Amber Smith
Ambra Tieszen
Amelia
Amelia Morton
Amelia O'Leary
Amelia Rose
Amelie Jarry
Amie Mattson
Amina Choudhury
Amirah Rivers
AML
Amrynth
Amy & Zoë Fischer
Amy andujar
Amy Avila
Amy Barnett
Amy Clark
Amy Dement & Catherine Adamson
Amy Dirks
Amy Fowler
Amy Gore
Amy Hackley
Amy Hilliard
Amy Malcom
Amy Osteraas
Amy R. Judd
Amy Silva
an avid bookworm
Ana Clara Fay
Ana Cristina
Ana Paula F. de Azevedo
AnaCrisi Skiver
Anastasia I Stolz
Anastasia Marie
Anders Scott
Andi Kozlowski
Andie "Bicho" Romanel Lopes
Andie Biagini
Andrea Calogero
Andrea Dillard
Andréa Fernandes
Andrea Grey Redman
Andrea Hasty
Andrea K
Andrea Lee
Andrea Lohafer

A SPECIAL THANK YOU

In addition to our amazing Kickstarter backers, we received immense help from the following:

SARAH STERN stepped in as proofreader/copy editor and has been an immense help to everyone in the anthology. She is a writer and artist and has carefully proofread every story in this book. If anything is wrong, it is entirely her fault. (Editors' note: No, it's not)

HIVEWORKS is a creator-owned digital publisher and studio that provided advertising & moral support. A number of the creators in the anthology are in Hiveworks and the financial support gained from it helped them to work on Valor. Thanks for the help!

Andrea Smith
Andrea YT Lin
Andrew Duff
Andrew G. Ryan
Andrew Green
Andrew J. Hayford
Andrew Murtha
Andrew Neale
Andrew Pam
Andrew Revere
Andrew Stevenson
Andrew Zimmerman Jones
Andy B
Angel Mishler
Angel Ramirez, Poseidon The Storm Bringer, Invisible Pen, & Of The Sea
Angela Rawlinson
Angela Rosa Takahara
Angeline C Burton
Angelique
Ani Mackie
Anis-Xayalith
Ann Bertram
Ann Doehring
Ann-Charlott
Anna A. Meyer
Anna Blanchet
Anna Cox
Anna Hagerty
Anna Jahraus
Anna Katharine Lamellas
Anna Noah
Anna Quinn
Anna Raftery
Anna Rance
Anna Studstill
Anna Tsardoulias
Anna Wiebelhaus
Anna Zoe Robot
Annalie & Elliora Gronberg
Annaliese
Anne H.
Anne Petersen
Annie Chartier-Grisi
Annie Pa
Annie Pollock
Annie Stoll
Annika Landberg
Annika Quint
Annika Roehr
Annika Stone
Annqueru
Anonymous Fan of Female Heroines
anotherfirename
Anthea West
Anthony Bonica
Anthony Gilberti
Anthony R. Cardno
Antonia Burns
Antonio M. Santos
Anya and Michael Scarpa
AO
aoife and ryan
Aparna Polavarapu
Apolinar E Padilla Junior
April Dennis
April G.
Aqualuft Games
Arachne Jericho
Aram Nimera Cyrthi
Araselle
Araswen
Argidy
Argonometra
Ari
Ari Harradine
Aria
Aria Grace Ilo Dot Rowa-Kie Perez
Ariana Maher
Ariana N. Dickey
Ariana Taylor
Arianna & Infinity
Arianna Lechan
Ariel A. Medoff
Ariel Allen
Ariel Coriaty
Ariel Mei Roberts
Ariel Rodgers
Ark Black
Arkady
ArkhamNative
Arleen Wolski
ARMDroider (Yutaka Suzuki)
Arnoldo G Rivas
Aron Lee Bowe
Arramel Syn
Arras M. Wiedorn
Arthur Kendragon
Åsa Palmborg
Asajii Reynolds
Åse Fahlander
Ash Brown
Ash Saraga
Ashercroix
Ashleigh Schmidt
Ashley Ballew
Ashley Berry
Ashley Burden
Ashley Carter~!
Ashley Clair
Ashley Jin Kim
Ashley Martin
Ashley Oswald
Ashley Protagonist Holmes
Ashli T.
Astrid Krivanek
Astrid María Stefánsdóttir
Astro Lark
Asuka-Marie
Aubrey Hobby
Aubrey L. Jeppson
Aubrey Morris
Auburn Kelton
Audra I.
Audrey H.
Audrey Redpath
Audrey Wayolle
auracel
Aurora Thornhill
Austin "Oh, I could tell you why the ocean's near the shore" Loomis
Austin Bantel
Austin Hager
Autumn Blaze
Autumn Crossman Serb
Avalon Warner-Gonzales
Avery Heart
AWS, LWS & AWS
B. Mack
B. Shropshire

B. Wadi
B.R. McSweeney
Bailey Gibson
Bailey Gorman
Barbara Lach
batSTAR
Bea Cayaban
Beatrice Matarazzo
Becca (Dino) Simon
Becca and Chris Shelton
Becca H.
Becca Hillburn
Becca Smith
Becky Allardice
Becky Bergmann
Becky Grutsch
Becky Lutz
Becky Moran
Becky Punch
Becky Thornton
Bees
Beezeeart
Belinda D.
Benjamin E.F. Callahan
Bernadette Royal
Bernardo Briceno
Berry
Beth Appelt
Beth Rheaume
Beth Yarde
Bethany Dyba
Bethany Morse
Beverly Marshall Saling
Bianca Christopher
Bianca Woods
Bis Thornton
Black Moth Man
Blackfish
Blaine "Belmont" Alleman
Blair Mueller
Blake Lee
Blake Sutton
blue
Blythe "Collie" Collier
Bobbie Paxton
Bogi Takács
Bonnie Lynn Wagner
Booze For Darla
Borialis & Evening Angel
Brad Drinnen
Brad Munn
Brad Phillips
Brad Steffen
Bradamante Smith
Braden Walker
Branchlaw
Brandon Duarte
Bree Cullum
Bree Nolan
Brenda Cantlay
Brenda Marie
Brendan "Heoru" Moeller
Brendan Carley
Brendan Hovan
Brendan S Stuart
Brenna Gardiner
Brenna S
Brennzz
Brett "DJ Archangel" Strassner
Brett Hiorns
Brett J. Brucklacher
Brett Stacey
Bri Spider
Brian
Brian Berling
Brian Cornell
Brian Huizingh
Briana Hughes
Brianna Novajasky
Briannah Lewis
Nikki Field"
Brianne Drouhard
Bridger Maskrey
Bridget K. Brule
Brittany Arnold
Brittany Drew
Brittany Dueker
Brittany LaLonde
Brittany Riles
Brittany Vitner
Brittany Wright
Brittney Gabbard
Brixton Watt
Brooke G. Lyonnais
Brooke Whitaker
Brooks Davis
Bruce Bevens
Bruna Guidini Santos and Deborah Bassi Stern
Bruno Guedes
Bryan Skow
Bryce Deary
Bryn Strahan
C. E. Lubsen
C. Ellis
C. Reyes
C. X. B.
C. Ziesman
C.A. Grenville
C.M.C & J.S.B.
C.M.S. Branting
C.S.R.
C.S.Rae
CA Moody
Cachoudoll
Cadance Lee
Cael
Caitlin "Weesnaw" Whelchel
Caitlin Belcher
Caitlin G.
Caitlin Lineback
Caitlin M. Taylor
Caitlin Mills-Groninger
Caitlin Naber
Caitlin Origoni
Caitlin Shaw
Caitlin Sido
Caitlin Stern
Caitlin Walker
Caitlin Wilson
Caitlin Yost
Caitlyn Aricelis
Caitlyn M.
Caley Ross
Cam Boyle
Camille Holmstedt
Camille Ruth DeCamp
Cammie
Campbell Family
Camwyn
Candace M.
Candice Bailey
Candice Guinan
Candice Meiners
Cara
Cara and Cathryn Wynn-Jones
Carey Pietsch
Carissa Badenoch
Carita Heinström / Kide
Carl Rigney
Carl Salbacka
Carla H.
Carla Luna Cullen
Carlos "The Los" Padilla
Carly Hamilton
Carmen V Urquilla
Carol J. Guess
Carol Pence
Carolyn Raufer
Carolyn Reid
Carolynn Hoople
Carolynne Beede
Carrie H.
Carrie Hausman
Carver Rapp
Casey Johnson
Casey M.
Cassandra Alvarez
Cassandra Feely
Cassandra Paris
Cassandra S.
Cassidy Percoco
Cassie "Artsykiwi" Pruitt
Cassie "The Egyptian" Lord
Cassie A.
Cassy Shaw
Castle K
Cat B.
Cat Bascle
Cat Leja
Cat Murphy
Cat Pauley
Cat Seaton
Cat Young
Catberks
Catharin Meadors
Catherine
Catherine Braiding
Catherine Crooks
Cathy Caulfield
Cátia Moreira
Catie Coleman
Catriona Mair Beamish
Cecilia and Naia Williams
Cecilia Palomo
Cecillie Lundsgaard
Cee and the Hellmouth
CEROU Cédric
Cesar Cesarotti
CF
Chandler Elizabeth Bullion
Chandra Tolmie
ChangnLeaf
Chantelle Walker
Charisse Tazewell
Charlene Harrison
Charley Bradford
Charlotte Ann McCleve
Charlotte DeVincenzo
Charlotte Marshall
Chasym
Chelsea Connor
Chelsie McNicol
Chereen G
Cheyanne Stinson
Chloé C. :)
Chloe Liotta-Jones
Chloe Nguyen
Chloe Prosser
Chloe Warden
Chris
Chris
Chris and Arianna
Chris Booker
Chris Demars
Chris Denchfield
Chris Keller
Chris L'Etoile
Chris Naz
Chris Olsen
Chris Oney
Chris Quinn
Chris W
Chrissy Baldwin
Chrissy Colli
Christa Dippel/Rivas
Christany Edwards
Christen Higgins
Christian Martin
Christian Melançon
Christie Anne
Christie Goulding
Christie R. Fremon
Christie S.
Christina 'VooDoo'
Christina Bartell
Christina Elliott!!
Christina K
Christina Major
Christina Retailliau
Christine Bertz
Christine Hipp
Christine L
Christine Osborne
Christopher Birnbaum
Christopher C. Cockrell
Christopher Krietz
Christopher Mangum
Christopher Teo
Christy Morgan
Christykins Norton and Teddy Bear Norton
Chyden Acar
Ciera Troy Dillard
Cindy Tea
Citty Cat
Claire de la Lune
Claire K. Campbell
Claire Mead
Claire Murray
Claire-Chan
Clara Hart
Clare Agrippina Belshaw
Claudia Berger
Claudia GIRARDI
Claudia Trajna
Clélie Ancelet
Clémence Mousset
Clémentine!
cleverwings
Clifford "Cliff's Notes"
Clifton
clockworkcrow
Cody Logan
Coleman bland
Colin J. Logue
Colin Keizer
Colin Stuart
Colleen Kao
Columbia Gg
Connie Chinn
Connie G.
Connor "The Roach" Richards
Connor Bartholomew
Contractor
Cora & Avery Sedenka
Cora Anderson
Coral Snowdeal
Cordell Finnson
Corey Self
Corey T Kump
Corian Grey Delaney
Corinna Cornett
Corinna Vigier
corny
Cory Hanson
Cory Louder
Cory Olesen
Cory Sherman
CosmicBiscuit
Courtland Eppelsheimer
Courtney Godbey
Courtney Gonzalez
Courtney Hahn
Courtney Wallace
Courtney Yu
Courtny Fenrich
Craig E. Petko
Craig Hackl
Craven
Cristi 'MOrgan' Simila
CrowFeatherWolf
Cryssi
Crystal F
Crystal H
Crystal K Knispel
Crystal M Rollins
Crystal Mora
Crystal Priestley
Crystal Young
Crystal-Bell (Ding-Ding)
CtrlAltFaceroll
Cuddly Tiger
Curtis Wenig
Cuttlefish of Cthulhu
Cwena
cybik
Cydney Tibrcel LaBarun
Cynamille
Cynthia Naoko Rowen
Cynthia Ramey
Cynthia Wood
D-Rock
D. J. R. Allkins
D. Ledge
D.W.
D.W.K. Crow
Dai Thompson
Daisy Calvert
daiyi
Dan Arrabal
Dan Delaney
Dan Eyer
Dan Pollack
Dan-Tran Cong-Huyen
Dana Fujita
Dana Rae
Dane and Jessica Salter
Danea Sears
Danella I. Regis
Dani Marie Kice
Dani McCade
Daniel "Shinji" Smith
Daniel B. Taylor
Daniel Carlyon
Daniel Kauwe
Daniel Kirrene
Daniel Lin
Daniel Maberry
Daniel McNamara
Daniel Monza
Daniel Romascano
Daniel Serbicki
Daniel Yokomizo
Daniela
Daniela Diaz Alonso
Daniela Margolis
Danielle Bates
Danielle Costello
Danielle Edwards
Danielle Keller
Danielle Lyn
Danielle Tu
Danielle Velez
Daninn James Zimmerman
Danita Rambo
Danny Baggett
Daphne Friedman
Dara Frances Covick
Dare Arowe
Darkor
Darryl Warcup
Dashima
David "Azzageddi" Farnell
David "The Geek" Kersey
David "Weimann" Karlson-Weimann
David and Stephanie Jones
David B-M
David Cannon
David Chuhay
David Dewitz
David E J Lees
David E Mumaw
David Goldstein
David Harvey
David J Thompson
David Lacorre
David Lawrence
David Michaels
David Peter
David Raynaud
David Sebastián
David Silberstein
Dawn Chester
Dawn Oshima
Dawnius
Dax Wain
Dayna Broder
DC
DC Fleming
DCLawrenceUK
Deanna Schiffman
Debbie & Becka Both
Debbie Barr
Debbie Chen
Debi May
Deborah J. Brannon
Deborah Low
Deborah Mary Blackman
Deborah Robinson
DeeDee McCaughan
Dein Dehouwer
Delisa E. Shepherd
Demming Norder
Denai Edwards
Denise Pirko
Denise, Kyle, Zoey & Paget
Derek Guder
Derek Lynch
Derek Song
Derrick Battle
Desiree Watson
Devan
Devin Jessup
Devin McKernan
Dexter Castillo
DGchans
Dian Garrett and family
Diana Gurfein
Diana Huh
Diana Lilwashu
Diana Paprotny
Diana Sprinkle
Diane E.
Diantris
Digital Skitty
Diogo Baquini
Dominic Quach
Dominique Giles
Don Elson
Donald Hopkins
Donelle Gryphon
Donovan Willett
Dooney
Dooplighost
Doreen Nguyen
Dorothy Ng
Dorothy Tokar
Doug Atkinson
Doug!
Dr. Kopong T. Limson
Draco
Drew Marie
Drose
Duncan A. Doherty
Duncan Baird
dydbunnies
Dylan "DRAGON BORN" Baggett
E Newbs
E. A. Morrissey
E. Panzenboeck
Ebbie H
Eden Brunson
Edith Sarabia
Edna Phong
Eduardo Redoschi
Edward Finos
Edward Gibson
Edward Woodstock
Eileen McLain
Elaine "TriaElf9" Tipping
Elaine d'Ete
Elan Carnahan
Elana Houde
Eldanaï Melain
Ele Jenkins
Elea Tiri
Eleanor Powell
Eleanor Stevens
Eleanor Webb
Elena Morgan
Elena Yi
Eli Landro
Elijah Martinez
Eliot Beer
Elisa Sguanci
Elisabeth Dufresne
Elisabeth Keene
Elisabeth Potsch
Elise Vézina-Easey
Elise Wall
Elissa Leach!
Elissa Sussman
Eliza Bowen
Elizabeth Adams
Elizabeth Baker
Elizabeth Cole
Elizabeth D. Cantu
Elizabeth Davidson
Elizabeth Friend
Elizabeth Hamilton
Elizabeth K
Elizabeth K-W
Elizabeth Neal
Elizabeth Parmeter
Elizabeth Patrician
Elizabeth Pau
Elizabeth Potter
Elizabeth Salazar
Elizabeth Sherry
Elizabeth Smith
Elizabeth Walkes
Elizabeth Wambheim
Elizabeth Williams
Elizardo [F&M] Valdez
Elle
Ellen Kaluza
Ellen Salt
Elletra Parnell
Ellie Hackney
Elliot McCollum
Ellipsis
Ellis Lin
Eloisa Marie Rodriguez (A True Child of the Sea)
Elsch
Elsydeon
Elyse
Em Higbee
Em Huff
em-j Rabbitwolf
Em's Mom
Emaline Burrow
EmelineBlack
Emilia Hald
Emilie Anderson-Grégoire
Emilord
Emily 'Reoakee' Newell
Emily Beauparlant
Emily Buck
Emily C
Emily C. Yolo
Emily Cannon
Emily Cheeseman
Emily Elizabethe Lewis
Emily Fetingis
Emily Hughes
Emily Jeanne Shults
Emily K
Emily Marchese
Emily Miller
Emily Nemes
Emily Norry
Emily Ott
Emily Parkerson
Emily Payne
Emily R.
Emily S. Cavalier
Emily Thomas
Emily Yang
Emma Cae
Emma Keefer
Emma Levine
Emma Lord
Emma M
Emma Rose Pringle
Emma Schroeder
Emma Spady
Emma Sterling
Emma W
Emmanuel François
Emmeline Pui Ling Dobson

Emmie Engqvist
Ena Enriquez
Enzel
Eoin T Wilmot
Eric A Jackson & Emilia Agrafojo
Eric A. Neish
Eric E. Torres
Eric J. Zylstra
Eric L.
Eric Menge
Eric O. Myre
Eric Sarrafian
Eric Webster
Erica "Vulpin the Ponyfox" Schmitt
Erica Canfield
Erica Duguid
Erica Loppnow
Erica Pantel
Erica Speegle
Erik & Dale Meyer-Curley
Erik Froment.
Erik Singer
Erika Pursiainen
Erika Sorensen
Erin "Lunulata" Smith
Erin and Patrick Cahill
Erin Beckmeyer
Erin Bradley
Erin F Lynch
Erin Fahey
Erin Goyins
Erin Harker
Erin Hewett
Erin Kacerovskis
Erin Magill
Erin McGill
Erin Moffitt
Erin Ratelle
Erin Riggsmith
Erin S. Mahony
Erin Subramanian
Erin Thompson
Erma, Anjelica, Francisco Talamante + Celeste Garcia
Esca Jensen
esmereldes
Essi Nopanen
Essie Bee
Estelle Hocquet
Esther Kim
Esther Lim
Etheral Snow
Etienne Campion Masson
Eva Fournier
Eva Newbold
Eva Schiffer
Eva Vanthomme
Eva Yonas
Evalyn-Averis McKinzie Baumgartner
Evan Behar
Evan Leeder
Evan Sutter
Evan Windsor
Evara Resvil
Eve Bolt
Eve Greenwood
Eve Trahant
Evelyn Crouse
Evie Talbot
Ewa Gawthrop
Ewan O'Sullivan
F. Evie, Archie and J.
F. A. Marti
Fabienne
Faith Stuart Williams
Fallon Leaf
Fantom Comics
Fatima Ahad
fawn!
Faye Bates
Fearful Symmetry
feikoi
Felicia DesJardins
Felicia Hudson
Ferunando
Fes Works
Feste
Finley S. Carter
Finn McInnes Stokes
Fiona
Fiona Erasmuson
Fiona Lynn Zimmer
Flávia Studart
Flore Voltaire
Floris van de Sande
Flynn the Cat
Fonzie Pants
"For K.L.&R"
Fran Stewart
France Trudel
Frances Jernigan-Clayton
Francesca Dare
Francine Françoise
Francis
Francis Lecours
Frank Reding
Frank, Corri, & the Monkey Crew
Franny Jay
Fred Hirsch
Friða Staksberg (Sorck)
Fumiki Nuss
G. J. Woods
G. Natt Raines
G.L. Day
G.L. Morrison
Gabe Phayt
Gabi
Gabriel Morgan
Gabriella Shigeta
Gabrielle Simmons
Gabrielle Taylor
Gail Crunkhorn
Galactic Guinea Pigs
Galena Ostipow
Galia B.
Gariabell Maa
Garuda Illo
Gary Gaines
Gary Phillips
Gemma Agar
Gemma Caswell
Gene A.
Gene Lee
Genevieve Alberti
Genevieve Hammang
Genevieve Schmitt
Genielysse Reyes
Geoff
Geoff Munn
Georganne Walters
George Geddes
George Rohac
Georgeann Muntin
Georgene Volintine
Georgia Frost
Georgia Pollock
Gerald Campbell
Gerry Cardinal III
Gibbs Moore
Giles Armstrong
Gillian Dawson
Gillian Kaplan
Gina Liu
Gina M.
Ginger
Gisela Peters
Gisele J
Giulia Barder
gobbldygook
Godahl
Golden Beard's Team
Goose Girl
Gordon Wyant
gowardfor
Grace and Nila Jacobson
Grace Anderson
Grace Antonas
Grace Gorski
Granny Pauline
Greg "schmegs" Schwartz
Greg Weir
Gretchen
Grizzly Bearon
guardian J
Gwen Phifer
Gwendolynn Amsbury
H. Rasmussen
Hadspen Blood
Hakkaeni
Halee M. Smith
Haley Hein
Haley Lynn Jo
Haley Parish
Haley Reeve
Hange
Hanna Biedron
Hanna Paquette
Hanna Pettersson
Hannah B
Hannah Beth Doney
Hannah Carver
Hannah D
Hannah Fattor
Hannah Ferrara
Hannah Haverkamp
Hannah J. Merchant
Hannah Karahkwenhawe Stacey
Hannah King
Hannah Schofield
Hannah Sloane
Hannah Taylor
Hannah Thoo
Hannah Walker
Happy Bunny
Harald Demler
Harry S
Hartchamber
Hassan Habib Lopez
Hassana Oyibo
Hatuli
Havard Sommervoll
Hayley Sandersen
Hayley Smith
Hazel
Heather & David
Heather & Sarah Silver
Heather A. Teel
Heather and Kay McCallum
Heather B
Heather Coates
Heather E. Pristash
Heather Hintze
Heather Hofshi
Heather L Telfer
Heather Maddigan
Heather Meadows
Heather Reid-Murray & Mike Murray
Heather Shanahan
Heather Swanston
Hector R Cerda Dyer
Heidi A. Wilde
Helen McNamara
Helen Owen
Helia
Henrik Lindhe
Hilda Serine
Hillary Froemel
Hitsugi Amachi
Hnubcig Yang
Hoh Yi Hui
Holly & Graham
Holly & Jeremy
Holly Booth
Holly Caddick
Holly Davis
Holly E. Atterbury
Hollz
Hope Anderson
Hope Henry-Chapin
Hope Nicholson
HOWGIRLS DOSPACE.COM
I Morel
Ian Connor
Ian McFarlin
Iarna
Icka! M. Chif
Iggy Koopa
Ignatius Montenegro
ILANA GALLARDO
Ilhja
Ilka
Imani J Dean
ImFarias
Imogen Pruthi
Indigo Pohlman
Ine
Irene Carolyn Shaw
Ironbite
Isaac Zerkle
Isabel Baker
Isabel Ryuu
Isabell Biggs
Isabella Blaine-Longo
Isabelle Potier
Isadora Tang
Isaiah Smalley
Isobel Wright
Istalir Aumer
Iván de Neymet Franco
Ivan P.
Ivan Velkovsky
Ivy Beth Gladstone
Ivy Hang
Izzy Mumm
J A Pickford
J A Wilde
J Cope
J Dungca & K Riehle
J Pharo
J Scott Knell
J Sprague
J. "Pedes" Piechowiak
J. Faddis
J. Godfrey
J. Kelly
J. Kenneth Riviere
J. Patrick Walker
J. Perkins
J. Quincy Sperber
J.A. Lauritzen
J.J. Irwin
J.L. Kimes
J.M. Cowan
J.M. Frey
J.Pawlik
jOllyolly
Jac Engelbrecht
Jacinta Molloy
Jack Vivace
Jackal Hollis
Jackie Abasolo a.k.a. "flowermiko"
Jackie McGarigle
Jackie Sherman
Jaclyn Gomez
Jacob Fisher
Jacob McClenny
Jacob Randolph
Jacob Wisner
Jacqueline M. Hanchar
Jacsebalon
Jada
Jade F Lee
Jade Harley
Jade JM
Jade Stewart
Jadine Lannon
Jaime C.
Jaime Wurth
Jaimes
James "Ven'Tatsu" Morgan
James Andrew Joyce
James C Holder
James D'Amato
James E Fallance
James Fletcher
James Grasselli
James Gray
James H. Murphy Jr.
James Olson
James Powers V
James Purves
James Riddell
James Schell
James Wilson
JamesH
Jamie Kinosian
Jamie Mayer
Jamie Winters
Jamieson
Jaminx
Jan Meiners
Jana Hoffmann
Janalee
Jane Mayhew
JaNeal M. Bartlett
Janell Biczak
Janelle Ludowise
Janerl
Janessa Ravenwood
Janice Lee
Janine Lisa Amberger
Janine Pham
Janna Kang
Jannika M
Jarrod C.
Jasmin Malik Chua
Jason "Muscadine" Crockett
Jason F. Broadley
Jason Leisemann
Jay Lofstead
Jayme Dale Mallindine
jc
JD Calderon
Jean Harrison
Jean-Philippe J
Jeanette Aprato
Jeanette Frost-Ramos
Jeanne
Jeannie Hisson
JeannieMarie DeMito
JEB
Jeff "JJ" Peterson
Jeff Bird
Jeffery Lawler
Jelena Vukcevic
Jemma Hill
Jen Barr
Jen Coster
Jen Edwards
Jen Hickman
Jen M
Jen Maccioli
Jen McGuire
Jen Memmolo
Jen Sheer
Jen Treese
JenMon
Jenn & Rose
Jenn Duncan
Jenn Wang
Jenna
Jenna Carlson
Jenna Stoeber
Jenna Zamie
Jennie Hazen
Jennifer
Jennifer A Spear
Jennifer Beale Cox
Jennifer Berk
Jennifer Brooks
Jennifer Cogar
Jennifer Dutton
Jennifer Ferragut
Jennifer Garnet Filo
Jennifer K. Koons
Jennifer L. Hykes
Jennifer M. Riddle
Jennifer Monsen
Jennifer Pease
Jennifer Ryan
Jennifer Thomas
Jennifer Thurmond
Jennifer Weber
Jennifer Wilson
Jennifer Z.
Jennifer Zyren Smith
Jenny (usagi) Krishnan
Jenny Appleby
Jenny Couture
Jenny McKeon
Jenny Wheeler
Jenny!
Jens Bejer Pedersen
Jeremie Lariviere
Jeremy Gwinner
Jerome Liao
Jerri Anne Kallam
Jerusha Wilson
Jesi Evans
Jess Idres
Jess Speir
Jessamine V.
Jessanne Sheppard
Jesse Jones
Jesse Taylor
Jesse Whyte
Jessica
Jessica - Nef
Jessica Alice
Jessica B
Jessica Benefiel
Jessica Berry
Jessica Blackshaw
Jessica Cantlope
Jessica Dawson
Jessica Ferreira
Jessica Fischer
Jessica G.
Jessica L.M. Taylor
Jessica Lynn Engelbrecht
Jessica Pacitto
Jessica Schulze
Jessica Scott
Jessica Sirkin
Jessica Stein
Jessica Vanderpol
Jessicca Moore
Jessie Crossman
Jessie EP Sun!
Jessie H.
JeweledNightingale
Jeydenise M.C & Angel M.V
Jherik
Jialing Pan
Jill Hughes
Jill McKinney
Jillianne Brown
Jim Arthurs and Crystal McDowell
Jim Coniglio
JJ
JJ Gavin-Prystupa
Jo PM
Joachim
Joanna Bendle
Joanna Claire Ormond
Joanna Shingler
Joanna Stegena
Jocelyn Fenton
Jocelyn Lopez
Jocelyn Oudesluys
Jocelyn Thresher
Jodi Goodin
Jodiann
Jodietron
Joe Fusion
Joe Lewis
Joe Penney
Joel G. "Monkey"
Joel Q
Johanna Solomon
Johannes Krampf
Johannes Luber
John 'johnkzin' Rudd
John & Stacy
John Cowdery
John Deemer
John F. Martin
John J Ostrosky Jr
John Komala
John L. Gehron
John MacLeod
John Rogers
John S. Troutman
John Sanchez
John Wesley Gordon
Johnahthon Skloss
Johnna Clark
Johnna-Claire
Joleen White
Jolene Follgard
Jon
Jon Fetter-Degges
Jon G.
Jon Stout (www.jonstout.net)
Jon Wratten
Jonas Humphrey
Jonas Richter
Jonathan "@TAComix" Davis
Jonathan "Chessboard Man" Barrett
Jonathan Foulkes
Jonathan H. Liu
Jonathan Hepburn
Jonathan Shaver
Jonathan Shepherd
Jonathan Singer
Jonathan W.
Jordan L. & Katie S.
Jordan LeAnn
Jordan Thompson
Jordan, Fatima, and Elliot
Jorden Varjassy
Jörg Tremme
Jorja Hung
josceline fenton
Josefina Hörberg
Joseph Civin
Joseph D. Compton
Joseph Randall
Joseph Stillwell
Josh
Josh and Kelsey Rogers
Josh L.
Josh More
Josh Vann
Joshua Munro
Joy Milligan
Joy Trujillo
Joy Vileniškis
Joyce Ann "inkgizmo" Martin
Joyce Barbarich
Joyce-Lynn Larocque
JT Hughes
Judith Owens
Judy M. Brenner
Judy Powers Murray
jujuthevuvu
Jules Y
Julia and James Ford
Julia B. Campbell
Julia B. Ellingboe
Júlia Besserman
Julia Christianson
Julia Francis
Julia G. Cowell
Julia Planes
Julia Summer Williams
Julia Vrtilek
Juliana Holzhauer-Barrie
Julie & Lily Stevens
Julie Dillon
Julie Lerche
Julie Levy
Julie Trenkle

Julie Vining & Colleen Ottomano
Juliet Critchlow
Jun & Sevi
Junelle Ward
Justin Kalinay
Justin Proffitt
Justine Creature
Justine Glass
K & T
K. C. Waddingham
K. E. Matthews
K. E. Muenz
K. Lau
K. McElligott
K.C.
K.H. Mercury
K.J. Rollins
K.S. Chasteen
Kaeley Slaney
Kaerien
Kaeti Vandorn
Kaija Harrison
Kailani
Kaitlin Callahan
Kaitlin Grignon
Kaitlin Saxton
Kaitlin Spangler
Kaitlyn Brady
Kaitlynn Schultz
Kali Van Nimwegen
Kamala Codrington-White
Kana
Kara Bell-Brey
Kara Prior
Karen
Karen Gunter
Karen Luk
Karen T
Karen Y.
Kari H.
Karin Lundberg
Karin Woodyard
Karina Masabanda
Karine Charlebois
Karo Myllymäki
Karon Keeney
Kasey Van Hise
Kasia Medyna
Kassandra and Karsten Dulgov
Kassandra Der
Kat Kan
Kat Knudson
Kat Martine-McEvoy
Kat Murphy
Kat Pillman
Kat Rowedder
Kat Spencer
Kata Kane & Ashley Altars
Katalina Vallez
Kate
Kate Ashwin
Kate Baker
Kate Flanagan
Kate Land and Chris Hutten-Czapski
Kate Naylor
Kate Nelson
Kate North
Kate Putnam
Kate Szollosy
Katelin Matthews
Katelyn Canez
Katelyn Cranmer
Katelyn McGill
Katerang*Reynolds
Katharina Gerlach
Katherine Angie Figueroa
Katherine Berhow
Katherine Brown
Katherine Carr
Katherine Donaldson
Katherine Fawcett
Katherine H.
Katherine Hempel
Katherine Kirby
Katherine Long
Katherine Malloy
Katherine Randall
Katherine S
Katherine Sugrue
Katherine Thornock
Katherine Yap
Katheryne Newman
Kathleen
Kathleen Amy Bradford
Kathleen Foley
Kathleen Kennedy
Kathleen Moyer
Kathleen Myers
Kathrine Yamamoto
Kathryn Albert
Kathryn Awesome
Kathryn Bernard
Kathryn Coyne
Kathryn Johnson
Kathy Falgout
Katie Bigham
Katie Cannon
Katie Cunico
Katie Dean
Katie Griffith
Katie McCamey
Katie McGuire
Katie McMahon
Katie O'Meara
Katie O'Neill
Katie Pearson-Wenger
Katie Randall
Katie White
Katrina
Katt M
Katy
Katy Lawson
Kay Shook
Kaycie D.
Kayla Kidwell-Snider
Kayla Witherow
Kaylee Hays
Kaylen R. J. Hughes
kayoche
Kaze
Keely D.
Keidy Zuniga
Keiralee B.
Keisha Luhrsen
Keith Andersen
Keith Bissett
Kel Lore
Kell Willsen
Kelley Jabr
Kelli Fisher
Kellie Ramirez
Kelly
Kelly Breswick
Kelly Delahanty
Kelly Gardiner
Kelly Griffith
Kelly Lexa
Kelly Stacy
Kelly Thompson
Kelly Weeren
Kelly Ziemski
Kelsey Anita Smith
Kelsey Avril
Kelsey Liggett
Kelsey Rousseau
Kelsey Werner
Kelseyica
Ken Catino
Ken Duarte
Kendra Rasmussen
Kennet Klokseth Pedersen
Kenneth A Graves
Kent Falconer
Keri A
Keri Bas
Kerrie Manning
Kerry Rae Morris
Kevan Mills - t.l.K.i
Kevin D. Bond
Kevin Julien
Kevin Monkhouse
Kevin Nguyen/Draiken Talkos
Kevin Tjen
Kevin Wong
Kezia Tubbs (TheKingKez)
Khi Kismet
Kiandra and Arwyn Brazeau
Kika Green
Killian Nelson
Kim Dufur
Kim Grimaldi
Kim Szurnicki
Kim Wincen
Kimber Hawes
Kimberley & Luc
Kimberly and Michael Lehman
Kimberly Maughan
Kimberly Pugh
Kimberly Towle (proud mother of Fiona Towle, the Viking-in-Training)
Kinaheso
Kira H.
Kira Parker
Kirk Becker
Kirra Thornton
Kirsten Lovstrom
Kirsten Uhde
Kirsty Pemberton
Kisai Yuki
Kit
Kit Seaton
Kitsune Heart
Kitty Hatfield
Kitty Williams
Kiyara Moore
Klara Leander
Knight Porter
Kniteando
Korina Skye
Kris Nielson
Kris Roland
Krishna Pterofractal Sivaranjan
Krista
Krista Barwick
Krista Foerster
Krista Majewski
Kristen "Xekstrin" Perez
Kristen Bernabe
Kristen Harvey
Kristen Ho
Kristen Keck
Kristie Strum
Kristin Hamilton
Kristin Maun
Kristina "Krispy" Peters
Kristina Eiberg
Kristina Rodriguez
Kristina Viggers
Kristine Herr
Kristine Macasieb
Kristjan Wager
Kristy Bourgeois
Krystal
Krystal Williamson
Krysten Mawson
Ksenia Winnicki
kts2008
Kurt Collins
Kyla Blythe-Prahl
Kyle Armstrong
Kyle Elizabeth Huck
Kyle Lenz
Kyle Rudy
Kyle Simons
Kyle Z. VanCourt
Kylea Kmiecik
Kyoul
Kyrstin Avello
L
L-M Jakobsen
L. Ann Ahlstrom
L. Liu
L. Mann
L.A. Christensen
L.C.
L.Modesto
LA Carlson
La petite fille
La'Sheema Babbs
Lace Lancaster
Lacey Van Nortwick
Laia FarrÉ JimÉnez
Laine L Ratsep
Lamson Nguyen
Lan Wang
Lance Bradford, Space Detective
Langdon Franz
Lani Aung
Lara Maria
Larissa Rüdiger
Larry Wentzel
Lau Mourão
Laura
Laura
Laura B.
Laura Bennett
Laura Humphreys
Laura Kertz
Laura Knight
Laura Lu
Laura O
Laura Pearce
Laura R.
Laura Sanchez-Reverri
Laura Schoenle
Laura Snow
Laura Tryon
Laura, David, Lily, and Maddy
Lauren "Wingéd Elf Girl" Sparks
Lauren Blanchard
Lauren C.
Lauren D.
Lauren Davis
Lauren Elizabeth
Lauren Fotiades
Lauren Gee Myers
Lauren Houser
Lauren Kraus
Lauren Maier
Lauren Oh
Lauren Perry
Lauren Scanlan
Laurian Bot
Laurianne Uy
Laurie A. MacDougall
Laurie Fernandez
Laurielle
lavvyan
Lawrence Bryans-MacGregor
Layla, Sabreen and Lori Hudaib
layleevj
Layne
Lea Urpa
Leafia
Leah
Leah "Taz" Helmrich
Leah Davis
Leah Goodreau
Leah Webber
Leah Weir
Lee Barker
Lee Onysko
Lee Rawles
Lee W.
Leigh
Lelia 'Nikki' Pittman
Lena Sawin
Leniad Kaznor
Lennie Olsen
Leonardo "El Leon" Fonseca
Lesen
Leshia-Aimée Doucet
Lesley S
Leslie Doyle (Angel Creations)
Leslie Trautman and Greg On
Leticia Rose Zaragoza
Lex Wilson
Lexi Corder
Lexi Sprague
Lexify
Ligia Serafim
Lilly Moore
Lilly Quinn, Simon David, Natasha, and Jacob Germany
Lily Corina Culbreath
Lily Horne
Lilyheart
Lilysea
Limtrot
Linda Orthner
Lindsay Robertson
Lindsey Aldred
Lindsey Fraser
Linnsey Nil
Lisa
Lisa
Lisa Polkosnik
Lisa Richelle Jensen
Lisa Yandell
Lissa Pattillo
Liz Duong
Liz Ellis
Liz Olhsson
Liz Tolleson
Liza J Dyer
Lizbeth Goodwill
Lizzie Martin
Lizzy M.
LJ Seashore - For 3 Little Fairies
Llyn Hunter
Lobster_writer
Logan Aerl Arias
Logan O. Uber
Loni Fiscus
Loralei Elizabeth
Lorelei M.
Lorelei Nguyen
Lori Flynn
Lori!
Lorna Doone
Lorson M. Poirier
Louis Kläy
Louise Anjou
Louise Williams
LTCool
Lucienne Brown, Ariel and Sierra Brown
Lucy Christie
Lucy Rose Muntersbjorn
Luke Eperthener
Luna De Sangre
Lydia Au
Lydia Hall
Lydia M.
Lydia Marlowe
Lydia Rogers
Lyle Coleman
Lyndsey N. Raney
Lyrinoir
Lys Stokes
Lyvia A Martinez
M
M Reed
M Walk
M. E. Gibbs
M. E. Oswald
M. Hobson
M. M. Owen
M. Sinclair
M. Tadashi Havey
M. Yang
M'lissa Wetherell-Moore, Rowan & William
Maarten Leo Daalder
Mabel Seyler
Mackenzie Raup
Mad Molly Wander
Maddalena Giovannini
Maddie Allen
Maddie Anderson
Maddie M Winograd
Maddie Tong
Maddy Young
Madeleine Michaud
Madeleine Price Ball
Madeline and Anna
Madeline Edmonds
Madeline Little
Madeline Yost
Madison Schrenk
Maggie Brevig
Maggie Houang
Maggie K Hedrick
Maggie Odd
Maggie S.
Maggie Vicknair
Maia Gillet
Maidenberg
Maile Hunter Murphy
Maiya Jack
Maja and Nina Urban
Maja Thalling
Maji
Makayla Arnold
Mako Kungfu
Malcolm Jamison
Malcolm Lee
Malloc
Mallorie Luna
Mallory Ely
Man Manto
Mandy Pederson
Manette
Manuel A. Vanegas
Mara Emmons
Mara Gebert
Maralyss
Maranda Morris
Marat Sverdlov
Marc Ball
Marc Christie
Marc Schablewski
Marcelle "Em-nat" Natisin
Marcus John Gray
Mareen Nobre
Marenka
Margaret A. Maloney
Margaret M. St. John
Margherita DiGregorio & Chris Legge
Margie Molnar
Margot Atwell
Margot Koval
Marguerite Kenner and Alasdair Stuart
Maria
Maria Blowers
Maria José de Juan Fraile
Mariana Albuquerque
Marie Anello
Marie Lupia
Marie Viala
Marie-Christine "Nawee" Bernier
Mariel Holm
Mariel Sorlien
Marietta G.
Marijke, Wyrd Queen
Marililc
Marilyn Levinson
Marin & Mal
Marina Mustieles Salvador
Marisa Grippo
Marissa "Blondie" Brice
Marissa Helmick-Nelson
Marissa Martinez
Marissa Meyer
Marit Aasen
Marita Jackson
Marjo M.
Marjorie Boyle
Mark A
Mark Anthony Campos
Mark Foo
Mark Hartsuyker
Mark Victor Ferrer
Marmæl
Marsena Ewing
Marten van der Leij
Martha Reeve
Martin and Marie Neubert
Marty Chodorek
Marty Martin
Mary
Mary Caldera
Mary Catherine O'Leary
Mary E Berson
Mary Rebecca Farris
Mary Sperry
Mary Ward
Marygrace Burns
Matt Harvey
Matt Kerre
Matt McClure
Matt Sawyer
Matt Spence
Matt Tichenor
Matthew Bannock
Matthew Bird
Matthew Cassar
Matthew Connolly
Matthew Cramer
Matthew Ellison
Matthew Finco
Matthew Gifford
Matthew Isom
Matthew Lind
Matthew Petrak
Matthew Whitehead
Maud Benard
Maud V
Max Zelinka
Maxime Roberge
Maxwell Heath
Maya Gadley
Maya O.
MDP
Meagan
Meagan Huber
Meaghan Healey
medras
Meeghan C. Appleman
Meena Echo
Meg (Marie-Eve Guindon)
Meg Brown
Meg Jones
Megan Ashley
Megan Bagley
Megan Coen
Megan Congdon
Megan Datoc
Megan E. Daggett
Megan E. Gardea
Megan Finn
Megan Grauer
Megan Harrell
Megan Hutto
Megan Izzy McGuire
Megan Jessup
Megan Rochlitz
Megan Rogge
Megan Waker
MegaZone
Meghan
Meghan Asaurus
Meghan Dornbrock
Meghan Hudson
Meghan S.
Meghann Stevens

Megs Brett
Meguin
Meibatsu-Prax Phuong Hong Au Nguyen
Melania "Fairymela" B.
Melanie DeJong
Melanie Good
Melanie Halley
Melanie Herscher
Melanie Hiller
Melinda Williams
Melissa Adams
Melissa Chellam
Melissa Cruz-Campbell
Melissa Elliott
Melissa Guillet
Melissa J. Massey
Melissa Nielsen
Melissa Trepanier
Melissa White
Melody Dunn
Melody M.
Memory Scarlett
Meredith Jeanne Gillies
Meredith Sweet
Meredith Tershel
Merissa Mayhew
Merlin Havlik
Merve Karasu
Meryl Friedman
MessaBunny
Mia Alcorn
Mica Bauhaus
Mica Low
Michael "4ier" Telford
Michael "Akemi" H.
Michael "Chaostraveler" Cencarik
Michael "Maikeruu" Pierno
Michael "Tanukitsune" Alonso
Michael Alparan
Michael Baker
Michael Brewer
Michael Ederer
Michael Feldhusen
Michael J. Allan
Michael Mair
Michael Martinez
Michael Mooney of the Crimson Fields
Michael Pattemore
Michael Staib
Michal
Michele Del Nobolo
Michelle
Michelle Chowning
Michelle Johnson
Michelle Paynes
Michelle Schmidlkofer
Michiko Ikins
Micki Galloway
Mid
midga
Midtime
Mikaela Yeversky
MiKayla "MiKayKay" Luke
Mike "Dragonsreach" Dodds
Mike Fischer
Mike Scudder
Mikhail "SnowyOwl" Malinin
Miko Kosi_ska
Millie A. Vender
Min
Mina
Minako Suzuki
Mindy Dai
Minna Sundberg
Miquette Thompson
Mira Era Chavdarov
Mira Ongchua
Miranda C.M. Farmer
Miranda Hutchinson
Miranda Steed
Miranda Thomas-Sailors
Miriam "Broeckchen" M˘bius
Miriam Ladd
Miryam Y. Ginsparg
MiSiU
Miso
Miss Hannah Marie
Missy Mirrix
Mitchell Family: Todd, Karen, Anneka & Colin
Mithrandir
Mittie Paul
Miyuki Hata & Diana Tantillo
mjkj
Mo Foley
Moa Frykholm
Moiya Heaton
Molisha Lovebit
Molly Hayden
Molly Mabel McEnroe Waters
Molly Ostertag
Mom
Monica Marlowe
Monica Perazzo
Moo_Indigo
Moore
Morgaine Newinter
Morgan Beem's biggest fan and older sister- Danielle Beem
Morgan Shandro
Morgan Sophia Barnett
Morgan Thomas
Mountainsoul
Mozamil Ashraf
Ms. Annie Nohn
Ms. Feminist
Mst
Munen
Mursen
MVES
Myisha Haynes
Myrntai
Mythee
Nadhirah Nadzri
Nadia & Julie Mundt
Nancy Anderson
Nanodot
Naomi Rath
Natala Helanri
Natalia
Natalia F
Natalia Seng
Natalie
Natalie
Natalie & Kyle Sprague
Natalie Ma
Natalie V? Ferguson
Natalie Vasco Lopez
Natasha
Natasha Hedeker
Natasha Weaver
Natasha West
Nate Welford-Small
Nathan Morrison
Nathan Rockwood
Nathan Silpakit
Nathaniel Ames
Natsuki Jinxing
Neal Frick
Neil Bredenberg
Nellie B
Nelson Zelaya.
Nerdier than Pi House
Nerukad
Nessie B
NewHeart
Nicholas A. Gonzalez
Nicholas Bolinger
Nicholas C Delaney
Nicholas George
Nichole Ward
NichT
Nick Czarnecki
Nick Jurun
Nicola "Nikofola" Young
Nicola Moretto
Nicola Morrison
Nicole C. Moy
Nicole D Teague
Nicole Dutton
Nicole English
Nicole LaCroix
Nicole Pasi
Nicole R. Stevens
Nicole Strang
Nicole Trudel
Niels Nellissen
Nigel Roberts
Niki La Teer
Nikki Perry
Nikki Ward
Nikki Zano
Nina Rachae Buie
NinjaKnight Comics
Nirven
Noah Ogata
noako
Noël Chrisman
Noella Grady
Nomun Neren
Noni Garcia
Nora Reiter
Nora Wainwright
Norma J. Lee
Norma JMB
Nsanelilmunky
Nudibranch
Nupur Maheshwari
Nuri Tal
Nurul Azriyani
Nykii Ryan
Nyssa Gilkey
Obake Style
Olanthanide
Oliver Perks
Olivia and Lucas Bevacqua
Olivia C. Bushey
Olivia Gillham
Olivia Lukawski
Olivia N.
Olivia P-G
Olivia Von Ruff
Olivier Bérubé-Fortin
Olivier TISSOT (FR)
Olna Jenn Smith
Omer
Ona Loots
Oniongentleman
Onneli
Optimystical Studios
Orlando Contino
OtherRealm Studio
Owen John Ryan
P.S.F.
Paige "Nova" Johnsen
Paige L.
Paige Luther
Paige Pozan
Pam Kryglik
Pamela Shaw
Pancakes in 3D
Pao-Lan Ladouceur
Papp István Péter
Parano
Parker
Pascal Tremblay
Pat Myers
Patricia Chan
Patricia Daguisan
Patricia Hendricks
Patricia J.
Patricia Langevin
Patricia Sanvictores
Patricia Vargas
Patrick McElroy
Patrick Mohlmann
Patrick Nelson
Patty Kirsch
Patty Saidenberg
Pau Doporto Gasull
Paul @DJNawtso Quick
Paul A. Brommer
Paul Biensan
Paul Freelend
Paul Strack
Pauline T. Luon
PaxEtRomana
Penelope Hutchins
Penelope Lattey
Penny
Pepi Valderrama (dePepi)
Pete Newell
Peter Chiykowski
Peter Christensen
Peter Hosey
Phaedra Collins-Tate
Phillip A Zepeda
Phillip Thomas
Phyra Sparks
Pierre Melancon
Pierre Piron
Pilar Guillory
Piper Gordon
Poppa
Pretty Jeff
Prince
Princess Kyoko
Priscilla Tov
Professor Stephen Candy
Prompt & Pleasant
psg
Psyche and Dante Lioncourt
Pug of Darkness
Queenortart
Quinnlyn and Kaia
R B Kersley
R.E.E.P.E.R. Men
Race DiLoreto
Rachael Heflin
Rachel
Rachel "Nausicaa" Tougas
Rachel Ayers
Rachel Blier
Rachel Brennan
Rachel Burress
Rachel Crisson
Rachel D.
Rachel Dowse
Rachel Fawcett
Rachel G.
Rachel J. Collins
Rachel King
Rachel L. Cohen
Rachel Lin
Rachel O.
Rachel Richey
Rachel Rivera
Rachel Smoot
Rachel Voorhies
Rachel W
Rachel Wade
Rae Elliott
Raegan Millhollin
Rafael David Suarez
Rafael Henrique Castanheira de Souza
Rafaella Angelica Nepales
Rain & Aidenn
Rambling Rambler Press
Ramsett
Randall Nichols
Randall Zimmerman
Randi Mason
Randi Misterka
randomanonym
Randy M Navarro
Raven Song
Ravensdance
Ray Nadine
ray powell
rc
Rebecca "DreamingKey" Lanning
Rebecca Bay
Rebecca Beets
Rebecca Blick
Rebecca Cerasoli
Rebecca Cowan
Rebecca Dixon
Rebecca Doyle
Rebecca Fenton
Rebecca Fleeman
Rebecca Hiatt
Rebecca Iglesias
Rebecca Johnson and Rowan Lanigan
Rebecca Jones
Rebecca Krentz-Wee
Rebecca Mitchell
Rebecca Rose Hepburn
Rebecca Rossiter
Rebecca Scott
Rebecca Wagoner
Rebecca Weiss
Rebecca Woolford
Reese Davis
Regina W.
Rel
Remadi
RÉmi Webster
REN
Renee
Renee Demers
Renni L.J.
Revek
RexCelestis
Rezi
Rhea Ewing
Rhianna Graves-Powell
Rhiannon Coath
Richard Appleby
Richard Gricius
Richard Heying
Richard L. J. Caves
Richard Pleyer
Richard Semple
Richards Family
Rick T. Dalby II
Rie Ma
Rigo Rich
Rika
Riley Rose
Rinkelle
Ripley Girard
Ripley Marvin
Risa Sumnwr
Rita Asangarani (Senorita)
Rita Rahr
Roanne Manzano-Roth
Rob a.k.a. theused182
Robert
Robert B. Elliott
Robert Bell
Robert Starling
Robert Summerill
Robert Usarek
Robin Andrea
Robin Cedar
Robin Hetzel
Robin K Herman
Robin L Bailey
Robin Parkins
Robyn Rewynd Williams
RockingRed VioletGirl
Rodney Romasanta
Rolan7
Romana Mayr
Ronald and Jordan Gregory
RoqueReptil
Rory Alexander Stilson
Rosalia
Rose
Rose Pascoe
Rose Turner
Rosemary A. Blodgett
Rosey Barber
Rosie 'Night Feather' Smith
Rosie Fan
rotmeister
Rowan Fae
RowenaTheWitch
Rowillage
roxyroxrx
Roy Barney
Roy Sutton
Roz Langley
Ruby A. MacPhail Stephenson
Ruby, Inara, and Maeven
Rue Nightly
Rukesh Patel (Lallipolaza)
Russell Dunk
Russell Nohelty
Rusty Rowley
Ruth Hunter
Ryan "Fly Rye" Hunt
Ryan Hall :)
Rylee & Jaice Keys-DuMars
S. A. Butler
S. Bermond
S. Kao
S. Stark
SaberSnowFlack
Sabia
Sabrina Rongen
Sabrina Strauss
Sabrina-Delphine S.
Sadie Kennedy
Sakura Brandi
sakuraember
Salazar-Goldman
SaLe
Sally Kearney
Sally Clair Evans
Sam
Sam Birnbaum @SMGB25
Samantha A. Patterson
Samantha Beinlich
Samantha David
Samantha Galvez
Samantha Griglack
Samantha Holloway
Samantha Knapp
Samantha M Derr
Samantha Marie Pavey
Samantha N.
Samantha Sadler
Samao
Sami
Sanchini Family
Sapphire
Sara A
Sara Austin
Sara Crow
Sara Glassman
Sara Kasari
Sara Kelsey McGee
Sara Martin
Sara Nalley
Sara Sestak
Sarah & Nathaniel Ball
Sarah A.
Sarah A.O. Rosner
Sarah Ann Head
Sarah Ann Lambrix
Sarah Arane
Sarah B.
Sarah B. (Madnmatter)
Sarah Barbour
Sarah Boas
Sarah Boyle
Sarah Brody
Sarah Carey
Sarah Coldheart
Sarah Conn
Sarah Doukakos
Sarah Forrester
Sarah Gondek
Sarah Greizer
Sarah Guichard
Sarah K Klipper
Sarah Keith
Sarah L. Robinson
Sarah Liberman
Sarah Lindquist
Sarah Moore
Sarah Morris
Sarah Ritter
Sarah Rohde
Sarah Schanze
Sarah Shorr
Sarah Stern
Sarah Tuck
Sarah W. Searle
Sarah_be
Sari Lomax
Saskia Hagemann
Savannah Houston-McIntyre
Saveroomforpi
Scarlett A. Lindblad
Scott Fogg
Scott K. Johnson
Scott Ringler
Scott Robert Lawrence
Scott Schaper
Scott Thompson
Sean M. P. Kennedy
Sean McCole
Sean O'C
Sean Westergaard Flindt
Sebastian Rives
Selena Marielle Johnson
Selina Eckert
Selina Maria Angotti
selkiesea
SGibbon
SGLee
ShadowTiger
Shahran Ahmed
Shakarean Hutchinson
Shamus Peveril
Shanna L. Brockmeyer
Shannon Elliott
Shannon M. Lynch
Shannon Moffett
Shannon Mun
Shannon Rae Lenfest
Shannon Williams
Shanti Chellaram
Shaun Kronenfeld
Shauna J. Grant
Shawn Prater
Shay L
Shego Caerndow
Sheila Rogers
Shelby K Alger
Shelby Lee
Sheyna Evans
Shi-Anne Colley
Shondra Snodderly
Shoshanna V. Mencher
Shuning Bian
Shweta Narayan and Nathaniel Smith
Siân Tukiainen
Sidowa Chiaroscuro
Siena Leslie
Sigurd Sigurd Brutus Motor
SilensVigilo
Silver
Sim Page
Simon Brilsby
Simon Poon
Simon Ward
Simone Shivani Miller
Siobhan Tate
Sirrob01
Sitthichok "Pomme" Khunthaveelab
Skeezix
sketchyfish@tumblr
Sky Oxford
Skye Morrison
Skylee Kay
Skyli Sketches

Skylore Miller (Aka: Renkore)
SlackerInitiative
Sleepingkiwi
Snow Wildsmith
Sofia Forier-Montes
Sofia Pacheco
Sofie Håkansson
Solarynis
Sonia Lai
Sophia
Sophia E. DeLeon
Sophia Hampton
Sophia McKissick
Sophia Nieuwboer
Sophia Revelis
Sophia Solo
Sophia W.
Sophie Forsyth
Sophie Raffan
Sorcyress
Soren Hughes
Sparkler Monthly magazine
Spencer Cotter
Spencer J Sale
spokespider
Spring Holbrook
Sprouts, Quinn :3, and Alex le Réveur
Squirmy & Squiddy
Stacy Ervin
Stacy Jones
Star-Poke
Starzy Rose
Stasia Archibald
Steen
Stefanie Battalene
Stefanie Craig
Stella Li
Stella Won Phelps
Stephanie C.
Stephanie Carey
Stephanie Catala
Stephanie Cross
Stephanie Forbes
Stephanie Jobe
Stephanie McMahon
Stephanie N.
Stephanie Smith @ Critterwings
Stephanie Swartz
Stephanie Wood
Stephanie, from West Virginia
Stephen Graham
Stephen Kilpatrick II
Stephenie & Solomon Walker
Sterling Walker
Steve
Steve Loiaconi
Steven R Meredith
Stevie Wilson
Stormphyre
Stregoica Zero
Stuart Chaplin
Susan Adami
Susan S.
Susan Tarrier
Susana Calderon
Susie Cummings
Sven Wiese
Svend Andersen & Celeste Mackintosh
Sydney
Sylvia Vale
Sysichi Crowe
T-Rexotron
T. Addelle Diedesch
T. Iwata
T.A. SImonelli
T.J. Fuller, Jr.
T.J. Smith
Tabi Joy
Tabitha V.
Tai C.
Tait Watt
Tala Rose Monroe
Talia Dutton
Taliabear
Tallulah JS
Tam An
Tamar "Thirteen" Conner
Tamara Havik
Tamara Shiels
Tamera Burnett
Tamereth
Tamey Paquet
Tania Gouaud
Tanna Borrell
Tanya Balasundaram
Tanya M. Burr
Tanya Taylor
Tara Clayton
Tara L Campbell
Tara Zimmerman
Tarryn Rae
Tasha "Nethilia" Campbell
Tasha Pealling
Tasha Turner
Tatterberry
Taylor Barkley
Taylor von Kugelgen
Tayls
Tazura Seiple
Teagan Caiach
Ted Anderson
Teeghan Doherty
Tegan L. Hendrickson
Tegan Murdock
Tenjou Utena
Teresa Brandall Tobias
Teresa Burton
Teresa Craft
Teron the Wolfhound
Terrana Cliff
Terri Johnson
Terri Oda
Tess Marie Thapalia
Thaddeus Callahan
Thainen
Thane Tuttle & Helen McGee
That Annoying Dirk Guy
thatraja
The Boehme Clan
the chimerical collective
The Echo Inside
The Girl at the Edge of the Ocean
The Lost Neko
the Madhat Kat
The Okamoto's
The Petty Family
The Pokos
The Sisters Evon
The Snaking Bend Rover Family
The Snapp's
The Snowed One
the swords family
The Teffera Sisters
the_Bear
Theodora Kofinas
TheWildRose
Thomas Borrmann
Thomas Bull
Thomas Chandler-Marshall
Thomas Faßnacht
Thomas G.B.
Thomas Jansen
Thomas Putney
Thomas Zilling
Thorn
Tianita
tib
Tiffany Jayde C Gontczaruk
Tiffany Masuda
Tiffany N.
Tiffany Shucart
Tiffany Sostar & Joseph Goethals
Tiffany Teders
Tiger Park
Tim Getty
Tim Huynh Le
Tim Kirk
Tim Meakins
Tim Trahan
Timothy Books
Timothy Lo
Tina Lee
Tina Moore
Tina Shaver
To Jocelyn Love Brobro
To our lovely granddaughters Layla and Serena for many hours of reading enjoyment
Tobi & Zoe Brown
Tobias Raifsnider
Toby M. Schreier
Tof Eklund
Tolkien
OverTwilight
Tom "Dreamshadow" Tjarks
Tom Clark
Tom Faller
Tom Joseph
Tom Sinclair
Tom Whiteley
Tommy Benoist
Tooi Gil (Blueberry-me)
Tony "Ayelmar" Herrington
Tony Eng
tonyl
Toot
Tori Fulton
Tori Larson
Totally Awesome Thelonia
Tova
Tracey, Morgan, and Lincoln Peer
Tracie B. Lucas
Travis Peterson
Trev
Trevor D. Garner
Trianna Valdes
TRickin
Trina Stec
TriOmegaZero
Trip Space-Parasite
Tumbleweed Williams
Turret
Twigs
Ty Liang
Tyler Chorneyko
Tyler Durden
Tyler E Riordan
Tyler Jones
Tymothy Peter Diaz
Tyrone "R3d_tiger" Queensborough
Tyrone "N-RyT" Wested
Ugly Dirt Box Universe
Uicker Family
Ulla Pritchard
Ursula Wood
Utarinsyis
V. Sheridan
V.Noche
Val
Val Marland
Vale B.
Valendra Venus.
Valentina Mauro
Valériane Duvivier
Valerie
Valerie "ShinyHappy Goth" Kaplan
Valerie Gillis
Valerie Mann
Valerie Starr
Vamsi
Vanessa dos Santos
Vanessa Satone
Vania Ding
Vasilina Vlasova
Vavia Avirom
Veronica
Veronica LC
Veronica T.
Veronika Knurenko
Viannah E. Duncan
Vibiana Tran
Vicki Hsu
Vicky Hanlon
Victoria M. Steidel
Victoria Shipway
Victoria Veziryan
Vidya Gopalakrishna
Vindarten
Violeta Venegas A.
Virginie McF
Vitality Magazine
Vivienne da Silva
Vivienne Jones and Rhiannon Jones White
VjbSeven
Vonny
Weathermage301
Welcome to TATE'S
Wendy Dziak
Wesley Robinson
Whimsy Angie
Wilda Greenbough
Will Emigh
Will Leight
Will Yeomans
Willa
Willa Sweeney
Willi Kampmann
William E Cook, Jr
William K.C. Yee
William L Frazier
William L. Lippitt
William Martin
William Mawdsley
William P. Davis, the Ringbearer
Wilmelyn Santos
Wilson Wyllie
Win Evans
WolfZombie
WOOLFE GAME
Wormwood
Wren Lee
Xaermas
Yaka
Yedda Saeaeske Koopmans and Hendrik Ype Jan Ringnalda
Yezbel & Chelsea Salomon
Yllaria
Yoko "Nytrinhia" Weaver
Yoshiya Rain
Yuliya and Olga Bas
Yunru Connie Sung
Yurii "Saodhar" Furtat
Z
Zach and Zeb Dezern Hauptman
Zach Schuetz
Zachariah Kull
Zachary A Chio
Zachary Jeffries
Zachary Lasater
Zachary T. Irwin
Zachary Vaughn William Rice-Morehead
Zahra F.
Zak Bryson
Zander
Zania Stone
Zaru
zavi
Zellie
Ziggy Bendek
Zina Hutton
Zinden Caffeine
Zine
Zoé Barnard
Zoe Hayes
Zoe Head
Zoe Knight
Zoe Maxine
Zoe Steinberger
Zoey Svitlychnya
Zoo
Zora Blade
Zuzanna Jarota-Lay

CREATORS

ISABELLE MELANÇON is a co-editor of ***Valor*** and co-creator/artist of ***Namesake***. She also is part of the Hiveworks administration team. She lives in Gatineau, Quebec, where she is on the hunt for fairy tales and lemonade worth her time.

MEGAN LAVEY-HEATON is a co-editor of ***Valor*** and co-creator of ***Namesake***. A transplanted Southerner who lives in Pennsylvania, she requires her partners in crime, at least two books at her fingertips, coffee, and a cat on her arm.

JAYD AÏT-KACI is an American-born, French-grown, Canadian-living artist that does too much work and gets too little sleep. Her favorite things include hedgehogs, astrology, and coffee. She can cook a mean pasta alfredo.

ELENA "YAMINO" BARBARICH is a freelance artist known for her webcomic ***Sister Claire***. Her hobbies include voice-acting, dancing in front of the mirror, traveling, posing for pretentious photos, and going on adventures with her wife, Ash.

A colorful, mysterious creature native to North Carolina, **ASH BARNES** writes the Missing Moments for ***Sister Claire*** and helps plan the comic's story with her wife, Elena "Yamino" Barbarich. Ash can often be spotted building dart frog tanks.

MORGAN BEEM is a Denver, Colo.-based comic artist, who loves all things fairytale, and has a particular soft spot for things a little creepy.

CORY BROWN is the writer and editor of ***The End***, a sci-fi-adventure webcomic. When he's not writing or at work, he spends time with his husband, August, and helps look after their energetic daughter. He also enjoys writing silly title text.

AUGUST BROWN is an illustrator with a daughter, who he hopes will one day love this anthology and draw inspiration from it. He devotes his time to ***The End***, but jumped at the chance to draw something that wasn't a spaceship interior.

MEAGHAN CARTER is a freelance illustrator and self-published cartoonist. Based out of Toronto, she works in the Comic Book Embassy studio. She is the author behind ***Take off!*** and ***Godslave***.

NICOLE CHARTRAND is a concept artist, illustrator and comic creator from Montreal. She makes art for video games by day, and comics in every other waking moment. You can find her near a game console or the nearest source of coffee.

KADI FEDORUK is the creator of ***Blindsprings***. She doesn't sleep, she doesn't leave her house, she may in fact be ... a vampire. Or just a sleep-deprived artist with too many jobs. (but totally a vampire)

TIM FERRARA is an independent writer and fantasy magic enthusiast. A full time knowledge-seeker, Tim's recent independent work can be found in ***Hana Doki Kira***.

CREATORS

SARA GOETTER likes to draw stories about girls, monsters, adventure and sometimes monster girls on adventures. When she's not drawing she's playing video games and worrying about her cat.

EMILY HANN is a graduate of traditional animation from Algonquin College. She works as a background art supervisor on various Disney TV shows. She lives in Ontario, with a man and three rabbits.

MEGAN KEARNEY is a graduate of Sheridan College's animation program and manager of Comic Book Embassy, a busy co-work studio. She shares her home with her husband, son, a handful of rabbits, and too much laundry.

MICHELLE "MISHA" KRIVANEK, creator of ***Alice and the Nightmare***, is a Seattle artist who studied animation in New York City. When not working on comics she can be found doodling or smothering her cat.

JUSTIN LANJIL is a self-styled artist, illustrator and designer. Wizard wasn't on the job opportunities list so for now there's happiness to be found in making a different kind of magic happen on the pages of comics.

ANGELICA MARIA LOPEZ is from Canóvanas, Puerto Rico! She's based in Los Angeles and is the artist and writer for ***Solstoria***, an all-age comic about a girl who wants to become a knight in order to save her missing brother.

LAURA NEUBERT is an artist, writer, and traveler whose goal is to tell a good story or two. She hopes that you enjoy the one she has contributed to this anthology, and hopes to make many more in the future.

ALEXANDRA SINGER is a part-time writer, full-time editor whose favorite activities include video games, baking, and studying random historical periods for fun. She lives in Connecticut with her two cats, wife, and too many books.

KATIE SHANAHAN is a cartoonist, animator and story artist from Toronto. Collaborating with her brother, Steven, she's drawn comics for the Flight and Explorer anthologies, and the Joe Shuster nominated fantasy-humour series ***Silly Kingdom***

STEVEN "SHAGGY" SHANAHAN is a writer of comics, editor of videos, and voicer of voice things. With his sister, Katie, he's made many short comics, as well as their series, ***Silly Kingdom***. He can be found mostly on the Internet.

ANNIE STOLL is a freelance graphic designer for folks like Lucasfilm and Art Director at Sony Music by day, Comic Illustrator by night. Also makes a mean pineapple upside-down cake.

JOANNE WEBSTER is a writer who lives in New Brunswick with her husband, surrounded by their fortress of trees. She mostly works with fantasy stories and fairy tales of all kinds, inspired by her surroundings.

CREATORS

Want to read more from the creators who contributed to Valor? Check out our work!

Isabelle Melançon and Megan Lavey-Heaton: Namesake (www.namesakecomic.com)

Angelica Maria Lopez: Solstoria (www.solstoria.net)

Annie Stoll and Tim Ferrera: Ode (www.odecomic.com)

Elena "Yamino" Barbarich and Ash "Summerlightning" Barnes: Sister Claire (www.sisterclaire.com)

Emily Hann: www.emilyhann.com

Jayd Ait-Kaci and Alex Singer: Sfeer Theory and Small Town Witch (www.littlefoolery.com)

Joanne Webster: eastofthemoon.tumblr.com

Justin Lanjil: justinworks.net

Kadi Fedoruk: Blindsprings (www.blindsprings.com)

Katie and Shaggy Shanahan: Silly Kingdom (www.sillykingdom.com)

Laura Neubert: The Light-Eaters (rosengeist.tumblr.com)

Meaghan Carter: Take Off (www.megacarter.com/takeoff)

Megan Kearney: Beauty and The Beast (batb.thecomicseries.com)

Michelle "Misha" Krivanek: Alice and the Nightmare (aliceandthenightmare.com)

Morgan Beem: molibi.tumblr.com

Nicole Chartrand: Fey Winds (www.feywinds.com)

August and Cory Brown: The End (www.endcomic.com)

Sara Goetter: Haircut (smgoetter.tumblr.com)